WHERE

EVERYBODY

LOOKS

LIKE ME

Amistad
An Imprint of HarperCollins*Publishers*

WHERE
EVERYBODY
LOOKS
LIKE ME

At the Crossroads of
America's Black Colleges
and Culture

RON STODGHILL

WHERE EVERYBODY LOOKS LIKE ME. Copyright © 2015 by Ron Stodghill. All
rights reserved. Printed in the United States of America. No part of this
book may be used or reproduced in any manner whatsoever without written
permission except in the case of brief quotations embodied in critical articles
and reviews. For information, address HarperCollins Publishers, 195 Broad-
way, New York, NY 10007.

HarperCollins books may be purchased for educational, business, or sales
promotional use. For information, please e-mail the Special Markets Department at SPsales@harpercollins.com.

FIRST EDITION

Designed by Janet M. Evans

Library of Congress Cataloging-in-Publication Data has been applied for.

ISBN: 978-0-06-232323-1

15 16 17 18 19   OV/RRD   10 9 8 7 6 5 4 3 2 1

To my dad,
Dr. Ronald Stodghill,
my first teacher, educator, and mentor

In all things that are purely social we can be as separate as the fingers, yet one as the hand in all things essential to mutual progress.

—Booker T. Washington, Atlanta Compromise Speech, 1895

Freeing yourself was one thing, claiming ownership of that freed self was another.

—Toni Morrison, *Beloved*

In all of us there is a hunger, marrow deep, to know our heritage—to know who we are and where we have come from.

—Alex Haley

IN ORDER OF APPEARANCE

Barack Obama,
President of the United States of America

Dr. John Silvanus Wilson Jr.,
President of Morehouse College

Dr. Ronald L. Carter,
President of Johnson C. Smith University

Renee Higginbotham-Brooks,
Howard University, Trustee Vice Chair

Dr. Bill Cosby,
Comedian and Philanthropist

Dr. John Williams,
*Former Dean of Morehouse Business
and Economics Department*

Dr. Beverly Daniel Tatum,
President of Spelman College

Savannah Bowen,
Student at Howard University

Johnny C. Taylor Jr.,
President and CEO of the Thurgood Marshall Fund

CONTENTS

President Barack Obama and Morehouse College president John Silvanus Wilson arrive at the all-male school's graduation ceremony in Atlanta, Georgia, where President Obama delivered the 2013 commencement address.

(Curtis Compton/Corbis)

INTRODUCTION

ON A SPRING MORNING IN ATLANTA, PRESI-
dent Barack Obama strode across the canopied stage at Morehouse College, the iconic all-male liberal arts institution tucked away in a gritty section of the city's southwest side. The president, recently reelected to a second term, had delivered many graduation speeches, but this address was decidedly different in audience and historical significance. Here, adorned in Morehouse's traditional maroon gown, stood the most powerful black man the free world had ever known, face-to-face with some of the nation's smartest, most ambitious young black men.

The applause was thunderous as the president looked out into the sea of faces. A distant voice called out from the crowd. "We love you!"

"I love you back," the president volleyed, the cheers rising to even higher decibels. "That is why I am here."

It was May 2013 and a steady rain was falling from ashen skies, but nothing could dampen the spirited mood enveloping campus during this momentous gathering; Barack Obama was, notably, the first sitting president ever to deliver Morehouse's commencement, and the first in the state of Georgia since Franklin Delano Roosevelt's at the University of Georgia back in 1938. Draped in silk and velvet academic regalia, Obama struck an almost royal portrait; the ultimate blend of humility and swagger that Morehouse Men had been chasing for more than a century. Yet the president demurred that this address to Morehouse's graduates was actually one of the greatest honors of his life, and went on to express his gratitude that, among the crowd of some ten thousand, several Atlanta dignitaries had shown up to share in the occasion. He pointed out, in particular, several esteemed locals, including the congressman and civil rights hero John Lewis and Atlanta mayor Kasim Reed, a Howard University graduate.

Sitting on the dais directly behind President Obama was Morehouse's newly minted leader, Dr. John Silvanus Wilson Jr. It was a proud day for Wilson, a trim, square-jawed intellectual and Morehouse alum himself (class of '79), who, prior to taking Morehouse's helm earlier that year, had weathered a rather rocky term as head of the White House Initiative on Historically Black Colleges and Universities. Founded in the early '80s during the Reagan administration, the agency aimed to strengthen the nation's black colleges, most of which had been born after the Civil War to educate some half million newly freed slaves.

But under Wilson, the agency that once toiled as a Beltway backwater in the shadow of the U.S. Department of Education seriously flexed its muscles, modest though they were. Instead of the cheerleading to which black college leaders were accustomed, Wilson took them to task. He challenged historically black colleges and universities (or HBCUs, as they are known) to prove the value of their education and the degrees they conferred, relative to mainstream universities, and for those who failed to do so, he even threatened to invoke a new set of performance standards, putting at risk the millions of government dollars the schools received each year. Wilson's blunt criticism and push toward accountability, no matter how fair and levelheaded, had given him a decidedly mixed reputation among black college leaders; there was, in some circles, praise for his willingness to prod those sleepy old institutions to spruce up their brand and performance, and for increasing funding of Pell grants and other college aid programs. But mostly, black college leaders were incensed by his aggression, blaming him—and President Obama for that matter—for what they viewed as turning back the clock on black higher education. Behind closed doors, and even publicly on occasion, black college leaders blasted Wilson as President Obama's bad cop, whose support for a series of regressive policies, most notably draconian new credit standards for financial aid, was choking the breath out of black colleges.

In essence, Wilson had arrived at Morehouse needing a public relations boost, and it came a couple of weeks into his tenure when the White House called and said President Obama wished to deliver Morehouse's baccalaureate address that spring. Obama's offer was nothing less than fortuitous, as Wilson was, in fact, gearing up to cut millions from the university's bloated budget, which included laying off dozens of administrators. Now, ensconced in the springtime pageantry of graduating Morehouse's 129th class, Wilson basked in his rare moment of redemption, looking on as his former boss Obama opened his remarks with some good-natured teasing; giving props to black women for compromising their hairdos in the rain and then chiding those graduates, in a class of five hundred, whose academic records left something to be desired. "Some of you are graduating summa cum laude. Some of you are graduating magna cum laude. I know some of you are just graduating, 'thank you, Lordy.'"

The president, of course, made sure to recognize the university's legacy of producing some of the nation's greatest African American thinkers and public servants—Morehouse had graduated civil rights leader Martin Luther King Jr., former Atlanta mayor Maynard Jackson, and former secretary of the U.S. Department of Health and Human Services Louis W. Sullivan, to name a few—but not without some lighthearted ribbing. "I am humbled to stand here with all of you as an honorary Morehouse Man. I finally made it. And as I do, I'm mindful of an old saying: 'You can always tell a Morehouse Man, but you can't tell him much.'" The quip brought more laughter.

But the burden of any leader is that their words, more often than not, end up beneath a microscope. The most scripted message can betray them; the platitude morphs into indictment, the observation congeals into criticism. Surely, President Obama must have anticipated his speech that morning would end up dissected, distilled, and analyzed to death. Surely he must have recognized the slippery politics of the moment, the gotcha paradox that could undermine his exalted presence even among his own kind.

The divisive moment came a few minutes into the president's address as his message—a kind of call to action, framed in tough love—left some in the crowd scratching their head and wondering whether if, instead, they were hearing a sly, ill-timed condemnation of a generation of black males.

"We know that too many young men in our community continue to make bad choices," President Obama said. "And I have to say, growing up, I made quite a few myself. Sometimes I wrote off my own failings as just another example of the world trying to keep a black man down. I had a tendency sometimes to make excuses for me not doing the right thing. But one of the things that all of you have learned over the last four years is there's no longer any room for excuses. I understand there's a common fraternity creed here at Morehouse: 'Excuses are tools of the incompetent used to build bridges to nowhere and monuments of nothingness.' "

Obama's point arguably could have been lost on this army of fresh-faced graduates eager to launch their careers or move on to graduate school. After all, these brothers were the promise of black America; young, against-the-odds go-getters who had proven they possessed the work ethic and smarts to earn something most black males in America would never attain. Wasn't the president preaching to the wrong crowd? Wouldn't a presidential pat on the back for a job well done, mixed with some soaring rhetoric about their bright futures, have been more appropriate? Obama had said nothing of the sort, for instance, to the Naval Academy's 2009 graduates. There he could have riffed on the virtues of honor and trust, and how recent incidents of rape, sexual harassment, and cover-ups at the academy were reasons to reevaluate their own character as they rose into the ranks of our military. Instead, he proclaimed: "This class is about to become the latest link in a long, unbroken chain of heroism and victory, a chain forged in battles whose names are etched in the stone of this stadium." Of course, Obama's white-bread academic pedigree—he earned his degrees at Columbia and Harvard's law school—made the admonishments, in many eyes, all the more suspect.

But in reality, the fact and spirit of Obama's message, audience aside, was hard to contest. If Obama's Morehouse commencement speech bespoke one of his signature "teachable moments," it was that America's black colleges—once gleaming citadels of African American cultural and economic progress—today face a crisis that threatens to upend more than a century and a half of advances in science, business, theology, art, and other fields. In fact, he may not have gone far enough. He could have said that if black colleges—heck, if black people—remained on their current course, they risked reliving the social and economic hardships that their ancestors had struggled to overcome. No matter, his was a blunt message rarely heard on the black college podium, where the narrative, when told, is typically a love story populated with heroes: entertainment mogul Oprah Winfrey (Tennessee State University), Nobel laureate author Toni Morrison (Howard University), scholar and activist W. E. B. Du Bois (Fisk University), Supreme Court justice Thurgood Marshall (Howard University), Spike Lee (Morehouse College), former NFL star Jerry Rice (Mississippi Valley State), and children's activist Marian Wright Edelman (Spelman College).

Today's black colleges are indisputably under siege, and in his speech that day President Obama, trying to navigate a minefield of race-based American politics, sounded at times like a fatigued general rallying a cavalry of listless, outnumbered troops. The context, though, was clear: the halcyon days of a rising black middle class were fast waning; in their place were conservative state legislators scheming to shut down or merge poor-performing public black colleges to save money; black college presidents, already struggling to keep school doors open, at war with officials at the U.S. Department of Education over steep funding cuts and plans to withhold federal support from poorly performing universities; and overworked black college faculty feuding with administrators over wage freezes and inadequate resources for teaching and research.

Obama's message at times was awkwardly contrarian for such a celebratory occasion. Yet, in truth, the president could not have picked a better audience or moment for it. More than any other institution, historically black colleges and universities represent the most critical black demographic. They form the main artery connecting to the heart of black America; all the social and economic organs that determine the promise and peril of the race begin and end at black colleges. If this is a critical time in the history of black colleges, it is precisely because these are critical times in the history of black people, and vice versa. For better or worse, HBCUs are merely institutional reflections of the people they were built to serve, their fortunes a bellwether for the state of the race. The cyclical impact, perhaps oversimplified, of black colleges and their effect on the culture may go something like this: the cumulative effect of African Americans' inability to generate real personal or institutional wealth over time has, among other things, resulted in black colleges lacking a dedicated pool of alumni or corporate wealth to tap for large financial gifts and endowments. Weak endowments at black colleges make education less affordable by driving up tuition costs, creating a generation of black people unprepared for the job market. Among the legions of unemployed are black males who ultimately end up cycling in and out of the criminal justice system or even dead. The elimination of black males from communities manifests in black colleges that are roughly 70 percent women and 30 percent men. That lopsided ratio of educated black women to men only lessens the odds of building strong two-parent black households and accumulating any real wealth, to name only two important factors.

"Well, we've got no time for excuses," President Obama went on. "Not because the bitter legacy of slavery and segregation have vanished entirely; they have not. Not because racism and discrimination no longer exist; we know those are still out there. It's just that in today's hyperconnected, hypercompetitive world, with millions of young people from China and India and Brazil—many of whom started with a whole lot less than all of you did—all of them entering the global workforce alongside you, nobody is going to give you anything that you have not earned."

President Obama's suggestion that a sense of entitlement was derailing young African Americans from reaching their promise in life was harsh but spot-on. And, unfortunately, it's among a host of other plagues eroding the rich history of these black colleges—institutions that have long embodied, protected, and promoted black culture. The president's condemnation could well have included greedy, corrupt administrators; an excessively materialistic culture that promotes violence and thug life, misogyny, and drug use; and an overarching devaluing of education. He could have ruminated overall about the travesty of watching the pillars of black economic and social advancement crumble after prior generations risked their lives to learn to read and write.

Instead, President Obama offered the nation's newest black graduates a simpler truth. "Nobody cares how tough your upbringing was. Nobody cares if you suffered some discrimination. And moreover, you have to remember that whatever you've gone through, it pales in comparison to the hardships previous generations endured—and they overcame them."

President Obama's prognostications proved hard to refute. A few months later, in the fall of 2013, a remarkable thing happened in American college sports. Grambling State University's football team refused to play its scheduled game against Jackson State University. The team's grievances were plenty, but it all came down to money—or rather Grambling's lack of it. Players complained that, among other things, the weight room was raggedy and unsafe; tiles jutted from the floor, a leaky ceiling caused mold and mildew and had led to staph infections. Players had practiced through summer on a field of knee-high grass in 90-plus-degree heat; they purchased their own Gatorade and Muscle Milk or drank water from hoses beneath the stadium. While the university president and athletic director traveled by airplane to away games, players endured painfully long bus trips; 14 hours from their northern Louisiana campus to Indianapolis, Indiana; 17 hours to Kansas City, Missouri.

The story made headlines because Grambling State University, a historically black college, once boasted a football program that was the envy of intercollegiate athletics. Football fans honored the memory of Eddie Robinson, Grambling's legendary head coach. During his fifty-six years at Grambling, "Coach Eddie" was among the winningest coaches in NCAA history and a hall of fame inductee. Coach Eddie also became synonymous with Grambling's other icon: the famous high-stepping marching band.

But here's what articles in such publications as *USA Today*, the *New York Times*, and *Sports Illustrated* failed to mention: Grambling's players were merely expressing publicly what insiders at black colleges have known for years; that the erosion—from locker rooms to dormitories to biology labs—had sunk to new lows that not only threatened the survival of these historic institutions, but the fibers that have supported black cultural values and mores since the first slaves arrived on American soil four centuries ago. It is hard to imagine a single greater threat to the future of African Americans than the demise of its higher education system. As the late black philosopher W. E. B. Du Bois, who taught briefly at Wilberforce University, insisted, a university education is less about breadwinning than "above all, to be the organ of that fine adjustment between real life and the growing knowledge of life, an adjustment which forms the secret of civilization."

Today, HBCUs are stumbling, in some cases, toward extinction. Once hailed as national treasures, the life force behind the black surgeon, engineer, painter, or poet is scraping hard to get by.

Some 104 HBCUs exist, starting east in Oxford, Pennsylvania, at such institutions as Lincoln University, and as far west as Texas Southern in Houston and Langston University in Langston, Oklahoma. Experts in higher education don't expect most of these schools to survive. Based on current trends, they expect that by 2035, the number of HBCUs will shrink by more than half—with only 15 of these actually thriving. Once-solid institutions such as Morris Brown College in Atlanta, St. Paul's College in Lawrenceville, Virginia, and Barber-Scotia College in Concord, North Carolina, have either lost their academic accreditation or are mired in bankruptcy proceedings.

Black colleges are not suffering alone; most institutions of higher learning are struggling against declining enrollment, eroding government support, and rising competition from for-profit educational institutions. But the push from state governments, many Republican-led, to close or consolidate public HBCUs seems all but certain to accelerate black colleges' disappearance from the landscape of higher education. And let's face it, it's hard to separate the prevailing rhetoric against black colleges from a national social climate that provides new evidence all the time of a nation given to devaluing African American life and culture generally, whether it's buried in the racist e-mails of a senior Sony executive, or a CNN broadcast from the fiery, riotous streets of Ferguson, Missouri.

The bedrock of any advanced culture rests in educating its citizens. *Where Everybody Looks Like Me* is an account—gathered through personal interviews, university documents, legal transcripts, articles, and other sources—of an epic struggle to save more than a hundred critically important American educational institutions from dying. This book intentionally departs from the rhetoric and posturing that dominates so much of the discussion these days around black colleges. Instead, it tells the stories of the people navigating the challenges; the new guard of black college administrators such as Dr. John Silvanus Wilson Jr. trying to breathe new life into dusty Morehouse College, and Dr. Walter Kimbrough, president of Dillard University (aka the "Hip-Hop President"), who took issue with black rap impresario Dr. Dre's $35 million contribution to an unprecedented $70 million gift to already heavily endowed, predominantly white University of Southern California; professors such as Richard Deering, a rambunctious white economics professor whose protests of poor management at struggling Wilberforce University led to the resignation of its president; a new crop of corporate-style leaders such as Johnny Taylor, chief executive officer of the Thurgood Marshall College Fund; and, of course, the students— the future of our nation—such as Savannah Bowen, an academic star at a suburban New York high school who, after some life-changing revelations involving her white classmates, chose to attend Howard University over the elite white universities courting her.

And then there is Howard University, the grand dame of HBCUs, which has had its own dirty laundry of weakened finances and allegations of mismanagement tossed into public view. What began as a Howard board trustee's pointed letter to fellow trustees expressing grave concerns about Howard's future exploded into a full-blown crisis for the university—one that resulted in the resignation of

Howard's president, Sidney Ribeau, and its chief financial officer, as well as a shake-up of its board. *Where Everybody Looks Like Me* offers an inside account of that controversy from the woman whose letter triggered it, Renee Higginbotham-Brooks, a prominent Howard alumnus and attorney who lives in Fort Worth, Texas. When her letter was leaked to the media, Higginbotham-Brooks declined requests from reporters to discuss the matter. For this book, however, she agreed to meet privately on several occasions to share her side of the events that put Howard in the headlines.

The sum of these compelling figures captures the crisis—and hope—at these schools. Even more, their stories offer a fresh view behind closed doors; from the dreams of a young Rwandan genocide survivor and biology major determined to become a dentist, to the private world of the boards of directors, the ranks of the black intelligentsia, and industry leaders at ground zero of the intense debate and fight to save these precious historically black colleges and universities—the backbone of America's black middle class.

It is common in discussing black colleges and their futures to lump them together, but the reality is that each is about as alike as rap mogul P. Diddy (who attended Howard University) and Tea Party activist Herman Cain (a Morehouse Man); in fact, some are private, while others are public; there are rural and urban; two-year and four-year; open enrollment and selective black colleges. Some boast law schools, medical schools, or theological seminaries. If black colleges share anything in common, it is that most of them began with some religious affiliation, from African Methodist Episcopal to Presbyterian in the post–Civil War 1800s, and were founded by abolitionists, missionaries, and liberal philanthropists who set up churches and schools aimed at educating former slaves and their children.

Where Everybody Looks Like Me chronicles what is arguably the most tumultuous moment in recent history for *all* HBCUs and the figures behind them. The harsh economics buffeting higher education has proven particularly rough on black college leaders; indeed, some would argue that the past calamitous couple of years have been a kind of watershed in their tenures, a turning point in which their decisions were either saving universities from imminent collapse or hastening their extinction.

Why will historians likely reflect on these times as a defining era for America's black colleges? Aside from the gridiron mutiny at Grambling State University, it's also a time when dozens of HBCUs, from Kentucky State University in Frankfort to Morgan State University in Baltimore, were forced to send home thousands of students due to steep cuts in federal student aid; when dozens of college presidents, from Howard University in Washington, D.C., to South Carolina State University in Orangeburg, to Southern University in Baton Rouge, Louisiana, were ousted from their jobs over performance concerns; when board search committees struggled to find talent to fill once-prime corner office positions; when criminal investigations were launched into university business offices, Alabama State University, Elizabeth City State University, and Morgan State University among them, for alleged corruption and unethical practices; and when black college boards themselves appeared, in many cases, inept and mired in political infighting.

The irony, of course, is that during this black college meltdown, our nation's president happens to be black. While Barack Obama himself didn't attend a black college, black college leaders had assumed that his leadership would improve the prospects—whether it was increased federal funding or stronger White House advocacy—

for their sagging institutions. But by President Obama's second term, many of these same leaders were openly criticizing the president and his policies as unsupportive, if not downright hostile, to black colleges.

My fascination with black colleges began shortly after I started working at one. I joined the faculty of Johnson C. Smith University, a small, private historically black liberal arts college in Charlotte, North Carolina, founded by the Presbyterians in 1867 as Biddle Memorial Institute. When I started, the university's president, Dr. Ronald L. Carter, a theology scholar with a penchant for South African fine art and exotic-skinned cowboy boots, was just settling behind the reins. A graduate of Morehouse College and Boston University, he had spent a decade working in South Africa's antiapartheid movement. Carter's vision was to refashion JCSU from a sleepy liberal arts college disengaged from the city's well-heeled political machine into a fully engaged player in issues of economic development, public education, and social justice that shape the landscape of the so-called New South.

But those ambitious goals collided hard against more urgent matters threatening the university's day-to-day survival; from plummeting student enrollment, to steep funding cuts, to heightened federal oversight. Time, he recognized, was running out. "It is too late for further warnings," Carter said. "To paraphrase Bob Dylan, you don't need a weatherman to see the gale force winds now swirling around us. The perfect storm is here."

Eleanor Roosevelt, a Howard University trustee and United States First Lady, bids farewell to students and faculty as they set sail for Norway, Sweden, and Denmark to present a repertory of three plays.

(Bettmann/Corbis)

CHAPTER 1

TO HOWARD, WITH LOVE

JUST RELAX, BROTHER. DIDN'T I TELL YOU I had this covered?

Renee Higginbotham-Brooks, the petite fireball attorney and longtime Howard University trustee, said the voice startled her; the familiar boardroom baritone cutting hard into her sleep that morning. She recounted the story sitting in the nook of her spacious kitchen in Fort Worth, Texas, the bright sun pouring across the swimming pool out back and then through wide rectangular windows. The house was quiet save for the autumn breeze rustling the groves of trees in her cul-de-sac. She sat at the table sipping her coffee and searching her memory for the moment, the exact moment, when she sensed that her beloved Howard University—and frankly black colleges overall—had hit a new bottom.

Everything'll be fine. Trust me.

Higginbotham-Brooks said she recognized that commando voice instantly as none other than Barry Rand's. Addison Barry Rand, the black corporate powerhouse whose admirers arced rainbow-like from Avis to Xerox to the silver-hairs of the AARP, over which, at the time, he reigned.

Higginbotham-Brooks was in her early sixties, fair in complexion, with a slight accent true to her small-town Southern belle roots in Martinsville, Virginia. Her voice was high-pitched and feathery, but she was not a delicate woman. She was tough, the sort who curses and coddles with the same bemused curl of her lips. Higginbotham-Brooks said that in her early-morning haze she, too, half-wondered whether the intrusive voice was merely her dreaming. The past few days, she recalled, had been rough. H. Patrick Swygert, Howard's longtime president, was retiring, and the board of trustees had been working furiously to not only identify his successor, but to keep Howard on course during the transition. In ways Higginbotham-Brooks had never imagined, her beloved alma mater, Howard University, had begun to stumble. Its finances were weak, student enrollment was soft, and the faculty—which hadn't enjoyed a pay increase since whenever—was becoming bitter.

To the casual observer, the erosion was virtually imperceptible, yet Higginbotham-Brooks saw clearly the dismal trend lines at Howard and in higher education generally; from skyrocketing tuition, to crushing student debt, to shrinking wages for graduates. She knew that Howard, more than ever, needed a leader capable of preserving and expanding the university's preeminence even during this time of broad chaos throughout higher education. Founded in 1867 and based in the heart of Washington, D.C., Howard University had produced some of the nation's most important figures, and she refused to stand idly by and watch such an august institution wither away.

Higginbotham-Brooks stood as she described her next move: how she stepped gingerly across the carpeted room of Washington, D.C.'s Fairmont Hotel, and how she found her worst suspicions confirmed. There on the other side of her hotel room wall, in the adjacent parlor, were the sounds of a kind of postgame celebration, she says—lots of conspiratorial chuckling and back-slapping between Barry Rand and Sidney Ribeau, who the previous evening had been tapped by the board of trustees as the future of Howard, the six-teenth president of the eleven-thousand-student university. Here is her account of the meeting:

Man, I didn't know if it was going to happen, Sidney Ribeau said. *I mean, I was sweating bullets there for a while. I didn't know if we were going to be able to pull this off.*

I told you not to worry, that I was going to make sure it happened, Barry Rand told him.

Higginbotham-Brooks heard a laugh, then a clap, and figured the guys were high-fiving. The moment sickened her. These guys were buddies; she knew the truth: Sidney Ribeau was the brother of Barry Rand's ex-wife. She had told Rand, warned him, when Ribeau's name came up at the start of this search process, that he should recuse himself. He claimed he barely knew Sidney. "He was just a kid when I was married to his sister," she recalled him saying. Barely knew him, huh? What a crock! It didn't matter to her that fellow trustees and presidential search committee leaders Colin Powell and Richard Parsons tried to clean things up, publishing a letter to the editor in the *Washington Post*. "Despite no communication between these two men in more than thirty years, Mr. Rand, upon learning of Mr. Ribeau's prospective candidacy, recused himself from voting," the letter said. "At our request, however, he participated in deliberations."

What Higginbotham-Brooks viewed as Rand's ethical breach—despite what anyone told her—didn't especially shock her. Unlike many of her swooning colleagues, she had never warmed much to Barry Rand. There was something about the man she didn't quite trust; that cocky, old-boy "how dare you question me" testosterone that nearly soaked through his pinstripes. She respected the man's professional record, which included, among other things, winning not one, but two coveted Malcolm Baldrige National Quality Awards during his days at Xerox. Sure, Barry Rand knew his stuff. "The man is smart as hell—there's no denying that," she said.

Her real problem with Rand was simply this: for the past couple of years, as chair of Howard University's board of trustees, his performance, in her humble opinion, had been plain lousy. Under his stewardship, she felt that Howard University had turned a blind eye to a storm of potentially life-threatening forces, from steep declines in federal support to falling enrollment to a money-draining research hospital. While Higginbotham-Brooks had not yet brought herself to express it, she suspected many of Howard's woes stemmed directly from Rand himself—or more specifically from what she viewed as his backroom style of governing.

Man, this was the best thing to happen for Paula and me, Sidney Ribeau said, referring to Howard's new First Lady. *We're so happy to get out of the boonies. You know, Paula's been going crazy out there in Bowling Green.*

Bowling Green, Ohio, population thirty thousand, was the Rust Belt town where Ribeau had been president at Bowling Green State University for the past thirteen years.

It's going to be okay, brother, Barry Rand said. *Now let's talk about your contract. How does this sound to you? Five years?*

Yeah, five, that's fine . . .

How about the money? It's like $597,000. But there's like fifty thousand for Paula to have this executive search firm to find her a job.

Man, Paula don't need no job. She's gonna be with me. Just put that fifty on the bottom line. Can't you do that?

Yeah, that should be all right.

The men carried on like this for several minutes, according to

Higginbotham-Brooks, one pal hammering out the compensation package for the other. Rand, for his part, declined to comment on Higginbotham-Brooks's version of events. Stacey Mobley, a Washington attorney and Rand's successor as board chair, acknowledged Higginbotham-Brooks's recollection of a clandestine negotiating session between Rand and Ribeau at the Fairmont Hotel. But Mobley, speaking on the board's behalf, characterized any such meeting as inconsequential. The board's compensation committee hammered out that deal, as was customary. Whatever suspicions she harbored were misguided, Mobley said.

Yet the longer Higginbotham-Brooks listened that morning, the more unsettled she became. She wasn't sure what to do about what she was hearing. She stepped over to the nightstand and from her mobile phone dialed another trustee, Wayman Smith, for advice. Smith, a former senior executive at Anheuser-Busch who had chaired Howard's trustee board prior to Rand, dispensed his advice quickly. *Call over there right now and tell Barry you hear every word he's saying. And tell him you need to talk to him right away. As soon as his conversation is over, you need to talk to him.*

Higginbotham-Brooks hung up from her call with Wayman Smith, took a deep breath, called the hotel operator, and asked to be put through to the parlor. Barry Rand picked up. *Barry, I'm in the next room,* Higginbotham-Brooks told him. *I hear every word that you're saying.*

There was a long silence and then Rand's response. *What?*

I said, I'm in the next room. They put me in the next room. I'm next door. I hear everything. I need to talk to you. As soon as y'all finish, I need to talk to you.

There was another long silence, followed by soft footsteps of the men stepping away from the wall over to the dining room table. Howard's trustees always stayed at the Fairmont for meetings, so Higginbotham-Brooks knew well how the parlor was situated.

Okay, he said.

A few minutes later, Higginbotham-Brooks's phone rang. Rand asked: *You want me to come over there?*

No, I'm coming to you.

By then, Higginbotham-Brooks had dressed. She unlocked the door leading into the adjacent parlor and strolled in. Ribeau was gone.

Barry, she said, *we gotta talk.*

Long before Renee Higginbotham-Brooks became the gadfly of Howard University, she was just another dyed-in-the-wool black college loyalist. Such loyalists generally subscribe to the notion that while American higher education favors the white and well-heeled, black college students can still flourish inside an old underground movement more interested in building successful black academies than integrating white ones. Through the years, these loyalists have grown to become a fierce, if underestimated, bunch—impressively ubiquitous in generation as in geography. Within their ranks are lawmakers in Washington, D.C., software designers in Silicon Valley, financial traders in London, preachers in Mississippi, teachers in Detroit, pediatricians in Cameroon, and mechanical engineers in Tokyo. They are feeble octogenarians living in Arkansas farmhouses and young B-boys strutting through Harlem. They stand as devout Christians, Muslims, Seventh-day Adventists, and atheists.

A self-proclaimed leader of these proud and few, Renee Higginbotham-Brooks champions most everything about black colleges. She relishes their small class sizes and intimate instruction, a student body representing every hue in the rainbow mixing it up with professors speaking a patois of high-minded theory and grandma's common sense. She cherishes the social scene, too; the fierce, brassy marching bands peacocking across football fields in brilliant, colorful formations, the pageantry of Greeks stepping and stomping with so much flair, bravado, and humor. And the friendships—yes, the friendships—sprouting in late-night talks in cramped dorm rooms and nurtured at weddings, births, and funerals, and seasoned into old age. Degreed black folk who didn't attend a black college missed a big, important aspect of black culture.

What frustrates Higginbotham-Brooks and other black college loyalists is how even the best of these schools lack cachet among most high achievers; how graduates of predominantly white institutions tend to snub their noses at HBCUs, without sufficient knowledge of their contributions. Of course, black colleges themselves are partly to blame for this image problem. All too often, the social scene at black colleges eclipses their intellectual legacies. Who knew, for instance, that Beth Brown, the late NASA astrophysicist, was a Howard graduate, or that W. E. B. Du Bois began forming his ideas about the "Talented Tenth" as an undergraduate at Fisk University, or even more recently that a couple of obscure black professors, Michael O. Ezekwe and Samuel E. Besong at Alcorn State University and Delaware State University, respectively, published breakthrough research on heart disease prevention through the ingestion of purslane plant leaves? Or that the chief architect of the Martin Luther King Jr. Memorial in Washington, D.C., was Deryl McKissack, the twin sister of Cheryl McKissack Daniel. The women are part of the fifth generation of McKissack & McKissack, founded in 1905 as the nation's first African American–owned design and construction firm. What's more likely to get talked about is how Erykah Badu, Bone Thugs-N-Harmony, and Big Sean ripped it at Howard's homecoming.

In February 2013, for example, a historic event unceremoniously unfolded on Howard's campus: for the first time in the university's 146 years, Harvard University's debate team traveled to Howard's campus for the competition. The event, held in Cramton Auditorium, was billed as "The Great Debaters," a playful nod to a film from a few years back starring Denzel Washington and based on the life of a Wiley College professor who in the '30s spirited his debate team to a national championship against Harvard University.

A snowstorm along the East Coast added a bit of drama: clad in their signature crimson blazers, Harvard's team hustled onto the stage just minutes before the debate's scheduled 3 p.m. start time, a near no-show due to a flight delay out of Boston. For ninety minutes, the students squared off over whether gun manufacturers should be held liable for mass killings and whether women should be required to sign up for the Selective Service System. As is customary in such collegiate debates, no victor was declared, and the event was measured along the lines of the respect, decorum, and intellect displayed by each team. "Howard can hold their own against anybody," Higginbotham-Brooks boasted. "We have always attracted some of the brightest kids in the world."

If Renee Higginbotham-Brooks boasts constantly about Howard, she had in recent years worried about her alma mater. It was her concerns, and airing them, that triggered the university's abrupt changing of the guards; her questions and then criticism of Howard president Sidney Ribeau's performance, her scathing—and mysteriously leaked—letter to fellow Howard trustees, Ribeau's resignation under fire, trustee Vernon Jordan's search for a new president, the selection of Dr. Wayne A. I. Frederick as the new president, and, of course, Higginbotham-Brooks ultimately losing her position as board vice chair for going rogue. The board would ultimately decide not to renew her contract, ending her eighteen years of service.

Reactions to Higginbotham-Brooks's crusade run the gamut. Some have praised her as valiant and courageous, while others dismiss her efforts as alarmist and self-centered. Both assessments harbor some merit. After numerous meetings and conversations with her, it is easy to understand doubts about the purity of her intentions; to be thrown off, for instance, by her self-described sense of modesty, yet see a track record that suggests relishing control over the levers of power. Higginbotham-Brooks is strategic always, and Machiavellian when necessary. She is also an unabashedly political creature and a name-dropper of the first degree. ("Oprah is a friend of mine," she is quick to remind folks.)

Attorney Stacey Mobley said the board not renewing Higginbotham-Brooks's contract was anything but vindictive; it was an attempt to bring new blood to Howard's new president, Dr. Wayne A. I. Frederick. While Higginbotham-Brooks had served the board admirably, Mobley believed that eighteen years was too long to remain effective. Under his board leadership, he would enforce the twelve-year maximum written in the bylaws. "If you've been on the board for more than twelve years, I think your independence starts to be affected," Mobley said.

In some instances, Mobley said he understood and even shared some of her views on Dr. Ribeau's performance. These times required visionary strategic leadership, especially in stewarding Howard's hospital, a community safety net that had become a serious financial burden. In some cases, Dr. Ribeau had not proven equal to some of these larger functions. "We're at a point where we're looking at and leveraging many of our assets, from real estate to intellectual property, in ways that provide revenue to the university so that we don't have to rely on tuition," he said. "But this is not an issue of HBCUs—this is an issue of American higher education." The board had been hashing out a plan to address these problems for some time, and Higginbotham-Brooks's leaked letter merely complicated and burdened the process, he said.

The most important issue was that Howard University was taking some hard, necessary measures to fulfill its mission, a mission more urgent than ever. "People tend to think that we don't need black institutions now that some blacks have their pick of white institutions, but this notion is completely false," he said. "HBCUs are as relevant today as they ever were. And it's our responsibility to do all we can to support them."

On this fact, at least, Higginbotham-Brooks and Mobley seemed to agree. And in this light, Higginbotham-Brooks's motivations seem to lean more toward noble than selfish; it is easy to believe that she pressed forward against her detractors with the university's motto, "Truth and Service," ringing somewhere in her spirit.

The conceit of America's black college is rooted in its tradition of producing first-generation graduates. But there is always some currency in lineage, and few boast a purer black college pedigree than Renee Higginbotham-Brooks. Both her maternal and paternal grandfathers were black college graduates; one from Virginia State University in its first graduating class, and another from Shaw University in North Carolina, before going on to Leonard Medical

School in 1909. As was common back then, neither of her grand-
mothers attended college. But Higginbotham-Brooks's mother studied at Florida A&M on a tennis scholarship in the early 1940s, more
than a decade before Althea Gibson's reign as the first black female
professional to win at Wimbledon. At least for a while, her mother
played basketball, too, until, as the story went, the white coach
called her a monkey and her mother retorted that he was a gorilla,
and was promptly put off the team. Higginbotham-Brooks's father
went to North Carolina Central University for undergraduate school,
and later earned a master's degree in chemistry from North Carolina
A&T State University, where he remained as a professor throughout
his career.

Higginbotham-Brooks delighted in sharing old stories about her
family's weekend ritual; getting dressed up in their Sunday best and
going to black college football or basketball games throughout Virginia and the Carolinas. She was merely a toddler, but she could
sense something special in these events; a camaraderie that felt like
family. The South was still deeply segregated and the tight knit-ness
of young and old rallying around their college students thrilled her.

Higginbotham-Brooks was still in kneesocks when she decided
she wanted to go to Howard University. Her family had spent that
summer of 1958 in Washington, D.C., so that her mother, working
on her Ph.D., could take graduate courses at American University
while her father worked on his master's at Howard. Higginbotham-
Brooks's grandmother joined them to watch over little Renee while
her parents studied.

Her parents managed to salve her hurt of being away from friends
that summer with the carrot that she, too, would be going to college
in Washington—a college that would teach her how to be a good

first-grader. They planned to send her to a preschool program at Howard, where the family would reside in faculty housing. Trouble was, when the family arrived they learned that the program was full to capacity. Higginbotham-Brooks was crestfallen as each morning she watched all the kids stroll by her window on their way to "college" while she stayed in the apartment with her younger sister.

But Grandma improvised. "We're going to have our own little school," she consoled. By day, Higginbotham-Brooks practiced reading and writing. During the evenings, Grandma would gather several other children from the neighborhood and take them to campus, where they'd run around for a couple of hours, through administration buildings, classrooms, dormitories. Once the kids discovered where Howard's president, Mordecai Wyatt Johnson, resided, they'd walk up to the big brick house and knock on the door. Sometimes Dr. Johnson would even come out and greet them with a few friendly words. The experience pretty much sealed Higginbotham-Brooks's future plans. "Well, you gotta be real smart to go to Howard," her father would tell her.

An exceptional student, Higginbotham-Brooks sailed through grammar and junior high school. During her junior year of high school, her family moved to Greensboro, where she attended the mostly white Page High School. During the summer before her senior year, she studied at the elite boarding school Phillips Academy in Andover, Maryland.

It was 1969, a time of tumultuous social change and racial upheaval; and the events around her, from the hippies of Woodstock to the fiery rhetoric of Eldridge Cleaver, an early leader of the Black Panther party, made her long for the tight-knit black community in which she had grown up. Like her white classmates, she visited many of the elite eastern universities; Harvard, Yale, Princeton, Brandeis, MIT. During those trips, she would search for a black face on campus and often came away disappointed. Higginbotham-Brooks applied to a few white universities, mostly to appease her teachers, but when she got a letter from Howard offering her a four-year academic scholarship, the decision was sealed.

In the small, decidedly modest world of black colleges, Howard University held a kind of snob appeal. Named after Oliver Otis Howard, a Civil War general who went on to lead the Freedmen's Bureau, Howard was chartered as a private university by an act of the United States Congress in 1867, the only HBCU to hold that distinction. Howard, dubbed the "Black Harvard," also boasted the greatest number of African American graduates with Ph.D.s in the country.

In contrast to most other black postsecondary institutions of that era, the university was founded with a commitment to graduate and professional education. Two years after its founding, Howard established the first black law school in the nation. Among the generations of black civil rights lawyers to graduate was Thurgood Marshall, who argued *Brown v. Board of Education* in 1954, a case that desegregated public schools; Marshall would become the first African American justice on the U.S. Supreme Court.

Howard University's student body is known for its fiery idealism. In the 1920s, for example, student activism over poor governance led to the appointment of Howard president Mordecai Johnson, and later, in the '30s, students engaged in widespread demonstrations against segregation and job discrimination by downtown Washington, D.C., retailers. In the early '60s, Howard students including Stokely Carmichael participated in civil rights protests sweeping across the South—a movement that would result in a student strike that shut down the university.

From the moment her parents dropped her off at Meridian Hill Hall, an old hotel being renovated into a coed dorm—many students slept in the lounge while waiting for their rooms to be completed—Higginbotham-Brooks loved Howard. "I didn't want to think about being anywhere else. We partied every night. What was amazing was there were all these people there who looked like me who were doing everything under the sun."

The social and academic energy at Howard was intoxicating, and all the exceptional role models—professors, administrators, successful alumni—made her feel like she and her class of freshmen were capable of doing anything they dreamed of, as long as they invested the hard work to achieve it. And make no mistake: Howard was rigorous academically. Higginbotham-Brooks performed admirably, if only because of the fear Howard University president James Cheek put in her heart during freshman orientation. "Look to your left and look to your right," he told his newest crop. "Only one of you will be here in four years. That's right—one of three will finish at Howard."

Higginbotham-Brooks figured out early on that she wanted to go on to law school. She understood a bit about the field, having worked starting at thirteen years old at her uncle's law firm—her uncle also happened to be a Howard graduate. She socialized quite a bit, but rarely at the expense of her studies. She refused to become like that cadre of girls who seemed to be more interested in finding a husband than studying. Howard had a terrific medical school and quite a few women were on the hunt for a future doctor, eating dinner at Freedmen's Hospital hoping to catch an intern's eye.

She was too busy trying to compete with Howard's international students, who accounted for nearly a third of the student body. Higginbotham-Brooks was a political science major and was astonished at how academically solid her classmates from Africa and the Caribbean, many the offspring of heads of state, were in discussions of international politics. They were simply better educated, boasting the equivalent of two years of college when they arrived as freshmen.

As it turned out, during her senior year Higginbotham-Brooks would herself meet a medical student at Howard. Clarence Jackson Brooks was a proud Texan from a long line of physicians who had gone to all-black schools his whole life; a black high school, and later Howard University for both undergraduate and medical school.

After completing Howard Phi Beta Kappa and magna cum laude in 1974, Higginbotham-Brooks attended law school at Georgetown University, graduating in 1977. She and Jack married and moved to Fort Worth, where she spent nearly a decade as a federal labor relations attorney before establishing her own law practice, specializing in personal injury cases. Her reputation as a smart and ferocious litigator on everything from civil rights to health care won her the attention of Ann Richards, governor of Texas, who appointed her to help turn around the Texas Alcoholic Beverage Commission, the state's scandal-plagued regulatory agency. Higginbotham-Brooks proved a scrappy adversary to the cartel of old boys who dominated the industry through graft and other payoffs. When Richards lost her reelection and Higginbotham-Brooks returned all her energy to her practice, she was flush with powerful new connections and a new legal specialty: municipal bond transactions. By 2001, her sole practitioner firm was among the top counsels in the eight-state southwest region, playing a major role in such bond issues as the Dallas/Fort Worth International

Airport. Boasting a sprawling staff servicing some 750 clients, Higginbotham-Brooks was making buckets of money, more than she could ever spend on herself. Still, she wanted to play on an even bigger stage. She decided it was time to pursue one of her longtime dreams: to become a member of Howard University's board of trustees, which throughout its history had attracted a pantheon of power players, including Frederick Douglass, Booker T. Washington, Theodore Roosevelt Jr., Mary Clark Rockefeller, William H. Taft, and Kenneth Lewis, to name a few.

Higginbotham-Brooks called her friend Wayman Smith, a senior executive at Anheuser-Busch and a trustee on Howard's board, and told him she was interested in joining. Howard's board is as prestigious as it is sprawling, at times with as many as thirty members, including student representatives as well as alumni. Joining Howard's board would, through the years, put Higginbotham-Brooks in the company of power players: Frank Savage; Colin Powell; Debbie Allen and Phylicia Rashad; Richard Parsons; Gabrielle McDonald, the first black federal judge in Texas and chief judge of The Hague war crimes division; Ken Lewis, CEO of Bank of America; Earl Graves of Black Enterprise; Doug Wilder, former Virginia governor; and former New York congressman Jack Kemp, who later served as secretary of the U.S. Department of Housing and Urban Development.

Ken Lay, CEO of Enron, came the next year; John Thain at Merrill Lynch, head of the New York Stock Exchange, joined, too. "You've got to get their attention, Renee," Wayman Smith told her. Higginbotham-Brooks decided that with her twentieth anniversary approaching, it was an ideal time to make a healthy donation to Howard. During the weekend festivities in D.C., she handed Smith a check for $20,000—a move that earned her a special acknowledgment during an alumni luncheon attended by several trustees and other heavy hitters at the university. The following year, as Howard inaugurated Patrick Swygert as their fifteenth president, Higginbotham-Brooks wrote the university another check—this time for $15,000.

Howard was not unlike most private universities in both its structure and governance, in that three entities were responsible for its overall strategy: fiscal oversight, curriculum, and student affairs. As is customary, the university's head honcho was the governing board, or trustees, which, among other things, presided over the university's charter, oversaw overall performance, raised money, and approved budgets. The board's most critical role was hiring and assessing the performance of the university's president, at Howard, Sidney Ribeau. As the institution's chief executive, Ribeau was charged with shepherding the university's academic and administrative bodies, fund-raising, and serving overall as the university's public face. Beneath Ribeau, along with students and administrative staff, was perhaps the university's most precious asset: the faculty, whose interests within a vast range of disciplines and departments were formally represented by a faculty senate, and in various committees.

Howard University's board of trustees was comprised of thirty-two members; three alumni elected by the Howard Alumni Association, two students voted in by the Student Government Association, and two faculty members elected by the faculty senate. The overall board selects members for the remaining seats. At the time, there was only one general seat open, and the actress and *The Cosby Show* star Phylicia Rashad was running for it. Higginbotham-Brooks didn't like her chances for defeating Rashad. "Girl, you know you can't win against Claire Huxtable," her friends told her. Higginbotham-Brooks's home life was anything but the Huxtables'. Her marriage was deteriorating, leading to a nasty divorce in which she and her husband stopped speaking. "We raised our children by fax," she said.

Pressing forward to gain an alumni seat on Howard's board, Higginbotham-Brooks reached out to her Howard classmates, alum throughout Texas and her home state of Virginia, and eventually scored a victory. Higginbotham-Brooks joined a board that was decidedly male-dominated; when she first joined the board, there may have been five women. Gabrielle McDonald, the chief judge at The Hague, half-joked to Higginbotham-Brooks: "Don't let more than five of them go to the bathroom at one time because they'll have a meeting in there."

Still, Higginbotham-Brooks quickly discovered her calling on Howard's board. She loved rubbing elbows with titans—global leaders who weren't window dressing but a real working board who cared deeply about the university. She loved watching Ken Lewis work his connections; he put together deals for Howard such as re-developing the adjacent historic LeDroit Park, or talking national politics with Colin Powell during board retreats.

Higginbotham-Brooks also figured out how she could stand out among her new high-powered colleagues. The board was about to embark on an ambitious capital campaign, a rarity for a university that historically depended on funding from about a $225 million federal appropriation. Over the past decade, that federal assistance was declining, and Swygert was gearing up to tap new funding streams.

Throughout her career, Higginbotham-Brooks had earned a reputation as a formidable fund-raiser back in Texas. The only way to succeed as a bond attorney was to be fiercely political, to find and court the folks holding the purse strings.

She became a kind of fund-raising go-to for black politicians running for mayor: she helped Lee Brown, former drug czar under Bill Clinton and police chief in New York and Atlanta, win the mayor's seat in Houston; Ron Kirk in Dallas; and Marc Morial in New Orleans. Surprisingly, Howard had never reached far outside the Beltway to ask for money in any organized fashion—despite the fact that Howard U. was loved by its alumni all over the country.

Higginbotham-Brooks invited Swygert to Texas, where she organized three fund-raisers. "I want you to see how money can be raised by just asking people," she told him. Richard Parsons, who was chair of the fund development campaign and vice chair, was more than happy to share the responsibility.

Two years and several millions later, the board's governance committee promoted Higginbotham-Brooks to vice chair. But things had changed dramatically since Swygert had retired in 2008. And mostly for the worse. In her view, Howard's president Dr. Sidney Ribeau was slowly running the place into the ground—and someone needed to press the stop button before it was too late. Where to start? Her list of grievances was so long. Even among black students, Howard wasn't attracting the cream of the crop anymore, as most were heading to predominantly white schools, seduced by generous scholarships.

There was the university's weakening financial picture. While Howard received almost $225 million annually in federal appropriations—the only HBCU to enjoy such funding—declines in enrollment and cuts in other federal student aid were taking a toll. There, too, was Howard University Hospital, which was hemorrhaging money in its noble—and entirely necessary—effort to provide a safety net for Washington, D.C.'s indigent. It irked Higginbotham-Brooks, too, that Ribeau had contracted Robert M. Tarola, a white guy with no previous experience in higher education finance—or as Higginbotham-Brooks saw it, no affinity to HBCUs—to control the university's purse strings. For a while, Higginbotham-Brooks had tried to keep her mouth shut, but she was deeply worried.

In retrospect, Ribeau's inauguration validated her view that he was a poor fit for the role. His predecessor, Patrick Swygert, was a thoughtful man who was a Howard alum, both undergraduate and law school, and known as always prepared. In Higginbotham-Brooks's view, Ribeau, on the other hand, was mediocre at best, lacking, in her eyes, the intellectual gravitas or pedigree befitting Howard's stature. Heck, the man hadn't even prepared a decent speech for his own inauguration. His message that spring afternoon in 2009 was a hackneyed derivative of Barack Obama's stump speeches for the White House: "Yes we can, yes we can! We can do whatever we want to do!" Higginbotham-Brooks recalled sitting there waiting patiently for Ribeau to utter anything substantive, cutting her eyes now and then to her friend and fellow trustee Vernon Jordan, who stared blankly ahead. Standing before thousands, Ribeau failed to offer up anything that resembled a vision for the world's best black university.

Behind Ribeau was his wife, Paula, who had already managed to raise eyebrows in Howard's back offices. The woman, Higginbotham-

Brooks had decided, was poised to make trouble as Howard's First Lady. Days before the inauguration, for example, she noticed that the printed programs had somehow omitted Whetsel, her first husband's last name. She ordered that the programs be changed, a small but pricey adjustment costing north of $50,000.

Ribeau's wife turned heads on campus, too. Occupying an office on the fourth floor of the administration building, she earned a reputation for appearing without notice at cabinet meetings, usurping the agenda with random thoughts and ideas. A theme of sorts was developing: back in Bowling Green, for example, Dr. Ribeau had come under fire when, in the midst of a hiring freeze, the university hired his wife for $66,000 annually for duties that, among other things, included accompanying him to work-related events. At Howard, when President Obama's First Lady, Michelle, came to deliver a talk, faculty and staff alike grumbled that Dr. Ribeau was conspicuously missing while his wife—he liked to refer to them as copresidents—happily stepped in. Once, during a board meeting, she appeared unexpectedly with a pack of students in tow who waxed for nearly an hour about how they spent spring break. The room, packed with such power brokers as Vernon Jordan, Richard Parsons, Douglas Wilder, and Kasim Reed, worked hard to conceal their displeasure with the hijacking.

At Howard's helm, Ribeau's judgment often raised eyebrows. Higginbotham-Brooks was still livid, for instance, that a few months back he had authorized paying $1.1 million in bonuses to senior-level university officials at the same time he had pushed a tuition hike. The bonuses—ranging in size from $97,000 to $522,000—came to light less than a week after Ribeau announced that the university's expenses had exceeded its revenues during the first half of the fiscal year and warned of several cost-cutting measures, including shutting down buildings during breaks and furloughs for faculty and staff. Outraged, the faculty senate fired off a letter to Ribeau, calling the bonuses "morally repugnant," an "affront to the integrity of the university," and a "slap in the face to the entire faculty who have been laboring under salary compression for a number of years."

Higginbotham-Brooks was scared, not just for Howard but for black colleges everywhere that looked to Howard as the benchmark. No matter what critics said, this view was set in stone: HBCUs were the backbone of the black community and the urgency to keep them healthy was real. We were letting our children down by not supporting these institutions, by not making smart financial decisions when the entire world of higher education was changing fast and furiously. If leaders of these institutions didn't act now, our children and grandchildren faced being left behind. She wasn't about to let this happen—at least not at Howard—and certainly not on her watch.

Stars of the sitcom *A Different World (from left to right)*:
Jasmine Guy (as Whitley Marion Gilbert), Lisa Bonet
(as Denise Huxtable), Marisa Tomei (as Maggie Lauten),
Dawnn Lewis (as Jaleesa Vinson-Taylor), and Kadeem
Hardison (as Dwayne Cleophus Wayne).

(Lynn Goldsmith/Corbis)

CHAPTER 2

COSBY, UNPLUGGED

AMERICA'S ONCE-FAVORITE DAD WAS ON THE line. It was an early weekday morning. "It's the Bill Cosby machine," the comedian announced. "Wake up, man! I wanna talk about these colleges."

It's tough to remember now, but there was a time when Bill Cosby seemed next in line to be carved into Mount Rushmore. He was so big, so pioneering, so damn likable that even black folks were willing, for the most part, to forgive what had become an embarrassing tic of sorts; a kind of media-induced Tourette's in which Cosby, often unprovoked, would take the stage and rant endlessly on modern black life in America—witty if not misguided assaults on everything from irresponsible black teen mothers, to gun-toting gangsta youth, to hyperethnic, hard-to-pronounce black birth names.

More recently, though, what has become painfully apparent, too, is the extent to which Bill Cosby, in these artful soliloquies, has skirted his own personal failings, foibles, and perhaps even criminal proclivities; which, no less, include an ever-growing list of women alleging that, starting as far back as the early 1970s, Cosby drugged and raped them. While Cosby has denied or declined to address the various allegations, and even his own 2005 court deposition in which he admitted drugging a woman with Quaaludes for sex, his many accusers recount incidents of sexual assault and abuse that contradict everything we had imagined about him.

And yet in the perennially fragile world of HBCUs, where good press and large dollars remain in short supply, Bill Cosby's fall from grace represents something close to an apocalypse. The black college doomsayer searching for a sign of imminent extinction can only relish the woes of Bill Cosby. However, few figures living or dead can boast the impact that Cosby has wielded across the black higher education landscape, whether it was the millions of dollars he gifted schools from his own pocket, or the millions he helped raise hosting HBCU fund-raisers, or the credibility he gave the institutions by simply sporting a black college sweatshirt through an airport.

Admittedly, there has been some suspicion about his agenda, an unsettling sense that maybe the man had become too rich, powerful, and detached to empathize and comment credibly on modern black life and its struggles. The fact that most had grown up in households that revered Bill Cosby as an entertainer, family man, and black citizen of the world started to become less relevant than his cultural shape-shifting; that the Jell-O pudding man, before our eyes, had morphed into the grumpy old sage and scold of black America. Like those kids on his '90s TV show, Bill was suddenly saying the darndest things. "What part of Africa did this come from? We are not Africans. Those people are not Africans; they don't know a thing about Africa. With names like Shaniqua, Taliqua, and Mohammed and all of that crap, and all of them are in jail."

Yet as unsettling as Cosby's transformation was to watch, Cosby's views on black people, and especially young black people, have undeniably shaped popular black identity. Fat Albert, Claire Huxtable, and even Little Bill are like bells in the black subconscious that cannot be unrung; not any more than yanking down the six Chicago Bulls championship banners from the United Center would erase from a hoop fan's memory Michael Jordan's soaring dunks. Even amid the scandals, it's unlikely that a generation of black folks can—or are even willing to—let go of their fond recollections of *A Different World*, that funny, socially conscious '80s sitcom set in fictitious Hillman College, Cosby's paean to black college life. The trials of Whitley Gilbert and Dwayne Wayne did more to attract black college kids to black campuses than those "A Mind Is a Terrible Thing to Waste" public service announcements ever could.

On this morning, Cosby was, surprisingly, focused in his sermonizing, explaining that he had phoned because of his concern for his friend Renee Higginbotham-Brooks, the controversial trustee at Howard University—"it's like a lynching" is how he put it. What was happening to Higginbotham-Brooks, he said, typified the malady afflicting HBCUs generally; a corrosion of goodwill and moral ethics among their leaders. These leaders had become a blight on institutions that represent more than a source of academic degrees for blacks—the institutions hold a kind of psychic power as well, the ability to inspire a kid out of abject poverty and into the top echelons of business, government, or entertainment. As leading cultural critic Ta-Nehisi Coates wrote in *The Atlantic*: "Howard has a way of inculcating its students with a sense of mission. If you are going into writing, you understand that you are not a free agent, but the bearer of heritage walking in the steps of Hurston, Morrison, Baldwin, Wright, and Ellison. None of these writers appear in *Insurrections of the Mind*. Howard University taught me to be unsurprised by this. It also taught me that writing was war. . . . When *The Bell Curve* excerpt was published, one of my professors handed out the issue to every interested student. This was not a compliment. This was knowing your enemy."

The result, in most cases, is also transcendent. "There is pride in education," Cosby said. "The feeling I get watching young people walk across that stage. I don't care if it's community college, high school, or what. There's a sameness in having achieved and conquered those academics." It is a refrain trumpeted among star HBCU graduates, whether it's Common, the actor and rapper (Florida A&M University), singer-songwriter Erykah Badu (Grambling State University), or actress Taraji P. Henson (Howard University).

Cosby boasts an arsenal of anecdotes and tall tales meant to inspire black higher learning. Many are brief and endearing, like the time he was walking through an airport and a black man, about forty, came rushing up to him. The guy, despite being loaded down by luggage, was eager to deliver a message to Cosby, to express to him how much he appreciated what Cosby was saying about the importance of earning a college education. He stood there proudly, a former college football player, now working as a businessman, as living proof of the value of education. "I asked, 'You're happy?' And he said, 'Yessir!' That's education!"

Cosby has always backed up his talk with cash. In 1988, for instance, he and wife Camille gifted Spelman College with $20 million, the largest donation to a college or university by African Americans and the second largest made to an HBCU. At the time, the gift represented roughly 50 percent of Spelman's endowment. What's remarkable about the Cosbys' gift is that neither attended an HBCU. Cosby himself boasts an undergraduate degree from Temple and a doctorate in education from the University of Massachusetts, Amherst.

Perhaps even more than HBCU alum, the Cosbys have proven to value the critical mission of building institutions of higher learning that afford black people access to worlds of opportunity historically shut off to them. Their gift essentially represented a kind of clarion call to other affluent blacks to address the funding challenges of black colleges and inspire all African Americans to value and support their institutions. For all its social idealism, racial desegregation brought with it the unfortunate by-product of plucking black enterprises of their talent and resources. As black customers flocked to partake in the once racially restricted white-owned establishments, black commerce and culture suffered; thriving black commercial districts in cities such as Tulsa, Atlanta, Durham, and Savannah dried up; middle-class resort communities such as Idlewild, Michigan, and Oak Bluffs on Martha's Vineyard struggled to stay alive. At black colleges, a tide of declining black enrollment, along with budget cuts from the federal and state governments and waning private donations, began washing away decades of gains.

Indeed, as far back as the '60s, Black Panther leader Stokely Carmichael had warned about the paradox of desegregation, the dangerous complacency borne from a false sense of inclusion. "We cannot afford to be concerned about the six percent of black children in this country whom you allow to enter white schools. We are going to be concerned about the ninety-four percent." Racial integration policies led to a gradual neglect of the very institutions that prepared blacks to attend traditionally white schools. Some have posited that the decline of black colleges is a testament to the success of American integration, but this argument starts to fall apart under the statistical reality that the majority of the nation's elementary and secondary public school districts are increasingly segregated along racial lines.

The reality is that America's black students still rely largely on black colleges for attaining advanced degrees, and most of these institutions, unfortunately, are in various stages of disarray—and in Cosby's view, their fall is nothing less than tragic. A higher ed scholar of sorts, Cosby talks a blue streak about the history of black colleges; how prior to the Civil War, blacks were prohibited by law from learning to read and write (the exceptions were Oberlin College in Ohio and Bowdoin College in Maine). How the turning point came in the middle and later decades of the 1800s when abolitionists, missionaries, and liberal philanthropists began setting up churches and schools that would educate former slaves and their children. "When you go back to when these schools started, they were called normal schools," Cosby likes to lecture, referring to early institutions established to train high school graduates on the norms and standards to become teachers. "The history tells you there were four corners and in the center, a dirt floor."

Cheyney, Lincoln, and Wilberforce universities came first, followed by some two hundred more before the turn of the century—generally governed and staffed by whites. The schools gained momentum throughout the South as amendments to state laws that required educating former slaves, and other laws such as the Second Morrill Act of 1890, or the Land-Grant College Act, provided federal support for state education of agriculture, education, and military sciences to blacks.

Black college towns were typically sleepy enclaves steeped in the pride of moving up the nation's social and economic ladder, albeit one that was racially segregated. Students, drilled on the refinements of proper speech and dress, wore a badge of honor among the town's blue-collar locals, while faculty enjoyed an elite status in the realm of preachers and business owners. "You see, education is the primary part of surviving," Cosby said. "In any place, and any person, whether you are brought to a strange area or you came on your own, you've got to become acclimated—and education is the key to that."

The real heroes were those early teachers, white and black alike, who sparked the imaginations of African American students, and groomed them to become scientists, physicians, engineers, artists, musicians, teachers, and ministers. Cosby praised them not only for their ability to recast mind-sets more accustomed to field work, but also for their commitment to doing so against the hard, oftentimes violent, resistance of white oppressors. "All hell was being raised from racists to keep them from teaching. But they continued on," Cosby said. "These were real civil rights fighters because they made sure that these young people had the knowledge that they needed to have. If you wanted it, they would give it to you—above and beyond."

This isolated yet aspirational culture thrived until 1954 when the U.S. Supreme Court ruled against "separate but equal" school systems in *Brown v. Board of Education*. The landmark decision opened the floodgates for blacks to attend nonblack schools, weakening HBCUs' stronghold on black higher education, values, and culture. The U.S. Department of Education estimates that HBCUs today award about 16 percent of bachelor's degrees to black students compared to 35 percent in 1976.

The problems these days transcend declining enrollment. The challenges are unfortunately more systemic, and can be laid mostly at the feet of leadership; whether it is personal greed and financial malfeasance, inept management, or overall disengagement from the needs of students and faculty. Cosby could cite a litany of examples, from Alabama A&M University, to Wilberforce University, to Texas Southern University.

Among the most recent HBCU collapses was Morris Brown College in Atlanta, which filed for bankruptcy protection in 2012 to stave off creditors holding $13 million in bonds and threatening to foreclose on the property. Founded in 1881 by members of the African Methodist Episcopal Church, Morris Brown was once known for successfully educating the poorest black students and sending them back to their hometowns as teachers. In recent years, the university has mostly stumbled: from its peak of three thousand students, Morris Brown's enrollment over the decades had plummeted to below forty, its football stadium and most of its buildings shuttered. The problems began back in 2002, when the Southern Association of Colleges and Schools withdrew the university's accreditation, citing gross financial mismanagement. The penalty came on the heels of two of its former administrators pleading guilty to embezzling federal student aid money in a kind of rob-Peter-to-pay-Paul scheme to fund the university's basic operating expenses.

"If you're black, there's an understanding, or used to be, that you're going to protect your black brother and your black sister," Cosby said. "We tend to think, if we get somebody black in there, we can trust that person. But that's not true. You've got black people putting their hands in the till, misappropriating where they're supposed to be spending the money. And in college education, one of the greatest things that we do! There's the duplicity; why are we attacking our own people? It's duplicitous. It's an attack on black people."

Cosby was standing on his old proverbial soapbox now. Extending his duplicity theme, he shared a story, a recollection from some town hall meeting he had recently attended. At the event, he said, an elderly black man rose in the audience and began talking about how white people have always thwarted the opportunities for black people to advance in life. The man, who hailed from a small town in Louisiana, spun a captivating yarn about racial segregation in his hometown, and the indignities he had suffered as a child growing up there. His words, spoken in an old-timer's southern drawl, connected with the crowd, and soon folks were clapping and coaxing him on. "He says there are small dirt roads that lead into downtown, where everything was white-owned. They own the theaters and they own the benches. And he says there was a grass area downtown and there were two fountains; there was a white fountain, which was polished and had flowers growing around it and it was clean. And you walked up to it and you turned on the spigot, and the water came out nice and smooth."

Cosby, pausing a moment for dramatic effect, then went on. "He said, 'Then I went over to the fountain marked colored and the pipes were all rusty.' And everybody said, 'Yeah!' And the man said, 'There was trash all around it, and the grass was full of weeds. And the poor little colored children would come up to the fountain and they didn't know which way the water was going to come out. It would shoot up their nose, in their face.' And everybody sort of nodded, like 'Well, that's the way it is.' "

Cosby, though, said he was frustrated by the man's tale, and even more so by the crowd's response to it. Why, he wondered, didn't the black town folk take matters into their own hands? He had been preparing to speak to the crowd about the proud legacy of civil rights leaders, of the importance of boycotts and marches and organized action to shift social paradigms. But after the man's story, he was compelled to ask a question: "I said, about these two fountains, 'The white man's fountain is clear and clean. Yours is filthy. Why didn't you clean up your own fountain?' And everybody laughed when I said this, but I was serious. I said, 'Where is it in our minds, where you think that is the *end* of something? Where is the message in that? We're talking about our school-children not getting the kind of teaching they should . . . all these things you're talking about that people *don't* have, that they *should* have, and yet you're sitting here in this room having this meeting.' I said, 'Get up!' And everybody just kind of stared at me. Nobody stood up and shouted, 'Yeah, that's right!' But they sure shouted about those two fountains."

There are, unfortunately, examples of African American universities not being trusted to properly tend our own. Consider the strange case of Hattie McDaniel's missing Academy Award, the first-ever Oscar awarded to an African American. Some time after McDaniel won the Award for Best Supporting Actress for her role as the slave servant Mammy in *Gone with the Wind*, Margaret Mitchell's epic Civil War novel, she donated the award—a stone-mounted, five-by-six-inch plaque (the statuettes would come later)—to Howard University. It's unclear when exactly the Wichita, Kansas, native donated the award; her biographer Carlton Jackson has said that it was toward the end of her life, as she was dying of breast cancer and began gifting valuable possessions from her estate. More recent research by W. Burlette Carter, a law professor at George Washington University, suggests that the Oscar, after spending years in McDaniel's home, was likely given to Howard by one of McDaniel's close friends, fellow actor and Howard alumnus Leigh Whipper, founder of the Negro Actors Guild, who had amassed an impressive collection of black entertainment memorabilia. What's less debated is that the Oscar was last seen on display in Howard University's fine arts complex before, at some point in the late 1960s, it disappeared.

That McDaniel's achievement was not universally embraced among blacks only compounds the mystery. Back then, African American entertainers were relegated to playing mostly the lazy simpleton and obsequious servant, and actors willing to compromise their dignity to accept such roles risked being frowned upon. This fact, more than forty years later, has led to the larger question for Howard of whether McDaniel's award was stolen or simply misplaced. Some have theorized that a group of Howard students, caught up in the fervor of the racially charged 1960s and offended by McDaniel's win for playing the racially stereotypical role, stole the Oscar and tossed it into the

Potomac River. But in her research, Professor Carter has come to regard the '60s social protest theft as little more than urban myth; she says the Oscar likely disappeared from the Howard drama department's glass encasement in the early '70s as new faculty were transitioning in and reorganizing the drama department, and perhaps not recognizing McDaniel's plaque as an Oscar, tucked it away somewhere obscure where it still sits out of public view, collecting dust.

Whatever happened to Hattie McDaniel's Oscar, the shameful tale tends to resurface whenever Howard is angling to house culturally important works. The most recent instance came when the university's famed alumnus and former faculty member Toni Morrison decided to donate her papers to Princeton University, where she has served as a faculty member for nearly three decades. The move sparked considerable outrage because Howard is considered to be a primary catalyst behind Morrison's illustrious literary career; the place that not only afforded her the opportunity to interact with such brilliant thinkers as Stokely Carmichael, a student of hers, but also where she began penning her first novel, *The Bluest Eye*.

Instead of Howard, Cosby pointed to a squandered cultural gold mine at Fisk University to make his point. Fisk, which sits on forty acres in Nashville, Tennessee, was founded in 1866 and counts among its graduates W. E. B. Du Bois, U.S. congressman John Lewis, and Nikki Giovanni. "How can Fisk not realize what they had in the art that was given to them? How can you waste these things?"

The art controversy at Fisk, which ended up in a rather byzantine, highly publicized legal dispute, actually boiled down to a fight over the cash-strapped university's right to keep its doors open by selling off a donated art collection. Back in the late 1940s, Georgia O'Keeffe donated her art collection in honor of her late husband, Alfred Stieglitz, a photographer, art dealer, and studio owner. Housed in the Carl Van Vechten Gallery, the oldest of two art galleries on the university's campus, the collection was donated to recognize the mission of the HBCU and included O'Keeffe's own iconic painting *Radiator Building—Night, New York*. In all, O'Keeffe donated over one hundred pieces, including work by Picasso, Diego Rivera, and Renoir.

But O'Keeffe's collection, which was appraised as half of the university's total assets, was bound to Fisk by the stipulation that it was not to be separated or sold. Based on that stipulation, the Georgia O'Keeffe Museum and the state of Tennessee's attorney general pushed to block the sale. In the end, the Tennessee Supreme Court decided to allow Fisk to sell a 50 percent stake to the Crystal Bridges Museum of American Art in Arkansas, which was founded in 2011 by Walmart heiress Alice Walton. In the agreement, Fisk compromised its right to permanently display the collection; the university can show it two out of every four years instead. Alice Walton also pledged $1 million to spruce up Fisk's display facilities after the university complained it lacked the funds to properly showcase the artwork. The deal was bittersweet; for selling off half of perhaps its most prestigious asset, Fisk took in a much-needed $30 million to fund its core operations.

In fairness, HBCUs were not alone in their woes. More than a century old, Sweet Briar College, a majority white, all-girls liberal arts school in the hills of central Virginia, announced it was shutting down, despite its $85 million endowment. With only seven hundred students, the board caved to looming pressures, from surging financial aid costs to campus maintenance, an overall tab of roughly $250 million to stay afloat. "I think the whole of American higher education is on the cusp of a state of flux that we have never seen, ever," said Jimmy Jones, Sweet Briar's president.

American universities were suffering across the board, and questions over whether a college education was even worth the money these days were becoming a common refrain. Overwhelmingly, Americans were getting weary of the increasing cost of college, which since the late '70s had soared 1,120 percent. That meant ponying up an average of $15,000 per year for a public college, and nearly $33,000 for a private college, according to a Pew study. As the study put it: "a child born today will need $41,000 a year for public college and $93,000 a year for private college at the current rate of growth."

Employers, too, were losing confidence. No matter the degree, college graduates these days often lacked the skills and preparation needed to be successful on the job. According to McKinsey & Company, less than 50 percent of the nation's employers considered the recent grads they hired to be prepared. These days, American colleges are not only scrambling to figure out how to survive, but how to graduate students who bring value to the workforce. Gone are those heady days after World War II when the millions of returning GIs on federally subsidized educations breathed new life into the nation's middle class. While the best students are still clawing their way into Harvard, Princeton, Yale, and other elite schools, most students wind up at colleges struggling against skyrocketing costs and declining quality. Just over half of these will actually graduate, putting the United States, along with Italy, at the bottom of the barrel of wealthy countries. Experts predict that once the baby boomer generation retires, the generations that follow will be less educated than their predecessors for the first time ever.

Cosby's crusade, though, was focused especially on HBCUs, which served the novel purpose of educating first-generation black college students—and the institutions' slow death was hurting him at his core. He ended his rant by telling me yet another story.

"I saw the answer," he said. "It was in a prizefight. It was a black kid fighting a Dominican kid. The Dominican kid had a left hook, and this black kid was boxing and moving in and out. He won the first six rounds. Then all of a sudden, in the seventh round, the black kid figured he was going to end it all with a knockout. Instead, he got caught with a left hook. And that started a whole two minutes of him grabbing the ropes, spinning backwards, looking like Charlie Chaplin. Finally, the bell rang and he sat down in his corner and his manager, who was also black, looked at him and said, 'Don't do that. Go back to your sticking and moving.' But this kid, heck, I don't know what he was thinking. You can't be sure of what he was thinking because he had just gotten hit in the head."

Cosby chuckled at the memory. "Anyway, black kid goes back out there and tries to knock the guy out again. But he got caught in the head again, and now's he's just sloppy. He kept falling, getting up, falling, and getting up. When the bell rings, he comes back to his corner and he sits down and the guy threw a handful of water from the sponge on his face and he said this, and to me this is as clear as a bell: 'It's not what he's doing to *you*; it's what you're *not* doing!'"

Cosby paused, and when he spoke again he sounded weary. "Look," he said. "Pay those professors. Give the students those scholarships, and put Howard in a position to have educated strong people. Put that hospital in a position so that we can, like Jews, have these shining examples of what we can do in medicine and in research. Not in driving all the way to New York City to have board meetings, charge it to the school, and come back. It is not only ridiculous, but it's accepted and it's duplicitous. And these people know they are guilty of it. They are making a fool and mockery of our schools, and so are the people standing by and letting it happen."

Students Laurah Pollnais and Dalicia Barker listen
to a lecture at Spelman College.

(Tami Chapel/Reuters/Corbis)

CHAPTER 3

EAGLES' EGGS

"MOREHOUSE COLLEGE STUDENT SHOT ON campus."

The headline, unfortunately, wasn't so shocking. After all, school violence happens these days, everywhere. But even in this bang, bang shoot 'em up era we live in, there was kind of melancholy in reading the news about Morehouse College. After all, Morehouse, the all-male powerhouse of higher learning tucked away on sixty-one acres in the 'hood of southwest Atlanta, was supposed to be, well, different from other places.

For more than a century, Morehouse College—or the "House" as it is known by admirers—has always existed in its own kind of parallel universe, a paragon of black enlightenment and progress. The shooting, suffice it to say, didn't exactly fit with Morehouse's wholesome, buttoned-down image. Or any black college, for that matter. Trot out those United Negro College Fund stats if you'd like: yes, HBCUs graduate more than 50 percent of African American professionals, 50 percent of public school teachers, and 70 percent of dentists; more than one-third of degrees held by African Americans in the natural sciences, and one-third of undergraduate degrees held by African Americans in mathematics are awarded by HBCUs.

But gunplay at venerable Morehouse was nothing if not red meat for HBCU critics, whose voices seem to be growing shriller by the day as they questioned the relevance of these schools in this modern "postracial" era. "There's no shortage of traditional colleges willing to give black students a chance," journalist Jason L. Riley has opined in the *Wall Street Journal*. "When segregation was legal, black colleges were responsible for almost all black collegians. Today, nearly 90 percent of black students spurn such schools, and the available evidence shows that, in the main, these students are better off exercising their non-HBCU options."

On the web, in real time, were standard images of urban discord: an ambulance, yellow police tape, throngs of young black men standing in the night. The scene—young black men huddled in pulsing white lights—had become American media's saddest, most enduring cliché, with gum-chewing, baby-toting black women sassing folk running a close second. There were details: during an argument over who played next in a pickup basketball game at the university gymnasium, Cornelius Savage, a Morehouse senior, was shot in the arm by a student from neighboring Clark Atlanta University.

The story, developing through the evening, included an antiviolence vigil in which hundreds of Morehouse students prayed for Savage's recovery. Among those gathered that night at the vigil was Morehouse's newly minted president, Dr. John Silvanus Wilson Jr. At fifty years old, Wilson was good-looking with sharp facial features, a thin mustache, and closely cropped graying hair. He looked, in fact, straight from central casting for the role of Morehouse College's eleventh president; physically fit, serious in temperament, upper-middle class in values.

On this occasion, though, Wilson looked mostly deflated. "Morehouse cannot be Morehouse if we are distracted by safety and security concerns," Wilson solemnly told the crowd. "Safety and security are a top concern for us because we know you have sent your sons to us so they can learn and be ready for the world, and they can't do that if they don't feel safe and secure."

In January 2013, John Wilson took the reins of Morehouse College, shrouded in questions of whether he was the right man for the job. Sure, in academic circles, he was viewed as a golden boy. His credentials were a hybrid of classic and modern; after graduating Morehouse in 1979, Wilson, the son of a Baptist preacher in Philadelphia, went on to Harvard, where he earned two master's degrees in theological studies and education, as well as a doctorate in education. He went on to spend the next fifteen years in various administrative and fund-raising roles at the Massachusetts Institute of Technology, and later moved on to George Washington University, serving for nearly a decade in several senior administrative roles.

Yet these experiences also gave him a worldview that detoured sharply from many of his black college contemporaries, who still subscribed to the old autocratic "teacher and preacher" paradigm that was once the lifeblood of HBCUs. Wilson strongly believed the days of the lofty scholar-leader had become ineffective and that, without visionary hands-on operators and fund-raisers, black colleges would continue crumbling toward extinction.

It was a harsh message for the black college brass, but it had been Wilson's mantra throughout his career, most notably—and controversially—during his previous four years as executive director of the White House Initiative on Historically Black Colleges and Universities. In that role, Wilson had essentially served as the Obama administration's bad cop, ruffling feathers as he proselytized about everything from the benefits of developing stronger online education programs, to holding HBCU leaders more accountable for their performances, to rationalizing draconian cuts in key federally funded student aid programs. It was the funding reductions, though, that sparked the most outrage, specifically the so-called Direct PLUS Loan program, created in 1965 and designed to make college affordable for students from lower-income households. In 2012, with scant public notice, the Department of Education raised the credit standards for these loans, and the change wreaked havoc on students at HBCUs, including Morehouse. As some seventeen thousand students were sent home, Wilson found himself on the firing line—and essentially became persona non grata among HBCU's higher-ups.

The result was a sizable population of HBCU leaders eager to share their own unflattering John Wilson story. Renee Higginbotham-Brooks, for one, told about a time a couple of years ago when she confronted Wilson after he had delivered a sermon at the Howard University chapel. She approached him because she had it on good authority that Wilson was considering doing away with Howard's federal appropriation, around $225 million annually. After politely introducing herself, Higginbotham-Brooks began questioning his motives regarding Howard University.

Wilson recalled the moment well; mostly, he said, because Higginbotham-Brooks's assertion was so far-fetched. Why would Obama, the nation's first black president, ever tinker with an appropriation that had been in effect for more than a hundred years? He also recalled that Higginbotham-Brooks didn't look convinced by his assurances, and invited him to appear at Howard's next regular board meeting to assure other trustees, which he did. Wilson never understood who would have told such a bold-faced lie, but he was glad he showed up and cleared the air.

If President Obama's delivering Morehouse's 2013 graduation commencement served as a kind of coronation for Wilson as a paragon of new black college leadership, the reality was that the bar had been set low. During more than five years at the helm, his predecessor, Dr. Robert Michael Franklin, is perhaps mostly remembered for instituting the famously ridiculed dress code aimed at, among other things, preventing Morehouse's growing ranks of openly gay students from cross-dressing on campus. As Franklin's policy stated: "Wearing of clothing associated with women's garb (for example, dresses, tunics, purses, handbags, pumps, wigs, make-up, etc.) is banned."

Wilson was aiming higher. The task of educating today's black male was arguably more difficult than ever. The road to Morehouse is riddled with stumbling blocks. Whether it's during the K–12 years, when black male students are more than twice as likely to be suspended from school than white students, or when they are ready to graduate from college (only 54 percent will do so compared to 75 percent of their Caucasian and Asian American peers), their reading scores are lower than any other racial and ethnic group. Upon graduation, black males account for only roughly 5 percent of all college students, while only one in six will graduate. Legions of others will populate the nation's prisons; nearly half of African American males have been arrested before turning twenty-three. Overall, some 1 million out of the total 2.3 million incarcerated today are black males; estimates project one of every three black men will be locked up in prison at some point during their lives, if current trends continue.

Graves Hall. That's where Morehouse graduates say it starts, the evolution of the iconic Morehouse Man. Time was, all the freshmen resided in Graves Hall, young black men from across the country. Some of them were legacy students born to wealthy or influential families, such as Martin Luther King Jr., who was third-generation Morehouse on his maternal side and second generation on his paternal side when he matriculated in 1944. Others were from lower-income families, proud to be the first in their family to attend college. No matter their social pedigree, the guys arriving at historic Graves had this much in common: up until that moment, they were usually the smartest black male in their group.

The hard truth is, if you're a young black man in this country and you've earned your reputation as anything other than being an outstanding athlete or musician, you may as well be a unicorn at your high school. Black boy academic all-stars are in the minority. If you look at student performance in percentages, there are disproportionately more black girls making good grades in high schools than black boys. What makes the Morehouse experience special is that for the first time, these guys are coming together with other guys who possess the same level of ambition, value, knowledge, and skill.

As one longtime Morehouse professor said, laughing: "You went there because you're smart and you're told that the school has a good academic reputation, and there's some opportunity to develop brotherhood. But then you get there and spend the first two or three weeks debating, debating, debating. Nobody can sleep. They're thinking, 'I used to be the only one smart, now everybody's smart. Not only is everybody just as smart, I can't convince them that I'm smarter.'" In other words, much of the so-called Morehouse Mystique derives from cultivating already smart, driven young men in a tradition of achievement dating back several generations.

Nobody loved Morehouse and what it represented to the American psyche more than John Wilson. He loved ruminating about the secret sauce that made families cry for joy when the acceptance letter arrived. But even Wilson, who boasts considerable oratory gifts, struggled to explain the unique transformation that young men experience upon admission to Morehouse. Questions of its DNA follow him everywhere. The Morehouse Mystique is just that—a mystique, Wilson liked to say. Therefore, by definition, it defies definition. And then, with a sly grin, he might add, "I hesitate to use the analogy, but it's a bit like pornography; you know it when you see it."

When I met with Wilson in his office at Kilgore Campus Center, he offered a deeper, if not at times strained, analysis of the Morehouse Man—and why he worried that the archetype was losing its luster in the modern world. The explanation shed light on the strong social consciousness of its graduates; such as the restless spirit of, say, Spike Lee, who isn't content simply making movies but also needs to take public stances on everything from gentrification in Brooklyn to the social value of a Tyler Perry film.

Wilson believed Morehouse was the most powerful brand ever created for black men, and that his stewardship would surely be scrutinized for generations to come. A casual stroll across campus suggested as much: around him, etched into the redbrick façade of lecture halls, dorms, and administration buildings, were the names of some of Morehouse's greatest figures.

Wilson credited two men, John Hope and Benjamin Mays, both of them Morehouse presidents, for building the famous Morehouse prototype. Installed in 1906, Hope was the first African American president of Morehouse College. A graduate of Brown University, Hope had insisted that Morehouse Men were distinctive from other black men during the racially oppressive 1920s in America, not only in their courtly manner but in their view of themselves. Morehouse students were not reflections of what the broader white society thought they were: intellectually inferior brutes most happy in recreation. No, they were socially conscious strivers always pushing to advance their community. Even more, despite the black male stereotype, Morehouse men were not angry. They were optimistic and dignified, and as such represented a new way of being black and American. Hope proselytized negotiating those racially charged times with integrity and pride, with an eye toward undoing the binds blacks lived under. His philosophy echoed the famous Claude McKay poem, "If We Must Die."

Morehouse's biggest star, though, was Benjamin Mays, who took the college's reins in 1940 and sharpened Hope's assimilationist message into a fierier brand. Mays challenged students toward activism, to live within their social consciousness—hence Spike Lee. No matter what field of study you chose, you had a custodial, remedial, corrective role to play because American democracy was in contradiction to the Southern racist system governing them. Mays mentored many students, but the most significant to the Morehouse brand was, of course, Martin Luther King Jr., who dubbed Mays his "spiritual mentor."

Wilson spun a compelling yarn about the Mays-King connection, about how the inquisitive King would follow Mays back to his office after Mays's weekly student addresses at chapel to discuss issues of theology and human rights; how Mays would hang out with King and family at their home, often for supper on Sunday nights; how after college, King would continue to turn to his mentor for support and counsel, whether it was during the Montgomery bus boycott or King's protests against the war in Vietnam.

But here was the rub for Wilson. Sure, King's legend had once been a magnet for thousands of young black men, including Wilson himself. Like countless peers, Wilson himself grew up in a home with two portraits on the living room wall: King and John F. Kennedy. Yet his younger generation of African American males was far less attached to that civil rights history. The best of them were heading to the Harvards, Yales, and Stanfords.

The numbers painted a bleak picture. When Wilson was a student at Morehouse, some 80 percent of African Americans in higher education were being educated inside of HBCUs. Today 91 percent of African Americans in higher education are being educated outside of HBCUs. That meant in some four decades, HBCUs had gone from educating 80 percent of black students to only 9 percent.

The numbers were even bleaker for Morehouse's target of college-bound African American males, where competition proved to be the stiffest if only because half of the African American males in the country don't even make it out of high school. What's more is that only a small fraction of the statistical anomalies who graduate high school are even interested in attending a four-year college, a real conundrum for Morehouse recruiters. The challenge for Wilson was to identify that portion of the sharpest African American males, convince them to consider Morehouse, help them find the money to attend, and then make them Morehouse Men by the time they left.

To that end, Wilson believed his personal legacy rested in beefing up Morehouse's value proposition in hopes of attracting students with other handsome offers on the table. Rather than waste time at luncheons and press conferences—as many other HBCU presidents did—bemoaning Washington's so-called war on black colleges, Wilson wanted to build a twenty-first-century university—with smart classrooms, streamlined business operations, a robust endowment. He wanted Morehouse, in other words, to enjoy the necessary safeguards that would prevent forces beyond his control, such as changes to the Direct PLUS Loan program, from putting Morehouse out of business overnight.

Wilson's thinking reflected a new guard in black higher education: HBCU presidents who essentially refused to be defined by a narrative of grievances. His views tended to coincide with Beverly Daniel Tatum at Spelman, Dave Wilson at Morgan State University, Ron Carter at Johnson C. Smith University, Walter Kimbrough at Dillard University, Harold Martin at North Carolina A&T, and a few others. Like Wilson, each of them understood the urgency of hauling the once-great—if now anachronistic—HBCUs into a new age or risk losing them all together.

Not a mile away from Morehouse College, Dr. Beverly Daniel Tatum, the president of Spelman College, was at her own crossroads. Within the decidedly mixed bag of black colleges, Spelman, founded in 1881 and the all-girl sister school to Morehouse, was viewed as a kind of bourgeoisie debutante, blessed with enough wealth and academic firepower to compete with the nation's best white schools. Only parts of that characterization were accurate. No, she wasn't fighting the Herculean battles, of say, Wilberforce University, which was struggling to retain its accreditation. But anyone who thought Tatum's challenges were trivial didn't know much about the state of higher education.

Spelman was, in fact, blessed with a relatively large endowment of $327 million, thanks to a history of largesse from such wealthy families as the Rockefellers, and in more recent years Bill and Camille Cosby. Still, Spelman's endowment paled against other similarly sized all-girls liberal arts colleges. The endowment, for example, at Wellesley College, a predominantly white all-girls school, was $1.8 billion. So the truth was that Spelman girls arrived anything but privileged—especially these days.

In fact, Tatum's reality was this: in Spelman's 134-year history, she was only its ninth president—and she felt all the pressure that came with the distinction. Spelman liked to pick leaders and stick with them, unlike say, North Carolina's Shaw University, which had been led by nearly a half-dozen presidents since the '80s. Tatum was a wonky clinical psychologist, fair-skinned with shortly cropped hair. She wrote a book, *Why Are All the Black Kids Sitting Together in the Cafeteria?*, that became required reading in higher education diversity circles.

When Tatum, who graduated from the predominantly white University of Michigan (her own parents were Howard graduates), took over at Spelman in 2002, some 30 percent of its students were Pell grant eligible, or requiring financial assistance. Today, that number has risen to 50 percent, a spike that occurred without Spelman altering its recruiting standards.

Spelman was still attracting students from top-quality high schools, but if you looked at the nation's population growth, trends revealed that single African American women were driving much of the nation's population growth. The result was that Spelman's pool of talent was increasingly born to parents who didn't go to college themselves, and many were from low-income families. And the kicker, all derived from census data, was this: 50 percent of all black families earn $40,000 annually or less. Only about 10 percent of African American families earned $100,000, and less than a percent made $200,000 or more. Spelman's tuition—a bargain in Tatum's eyes, compared to competitors—hovered at $37,000 and was out of reach for Spelman's target student.

That simple arithmetic was Tatum's albatross. Obviously, she couldn't give away a Spelman education, which, in her view, was already priced far below market value. In today's world of small liberal arts colleges, any tuition under $40,000 per year was a bargain. Tuitions of predominantly white schools of similar quality were nearly double Spelman's. During a recent meeting in Washington, D.C., Tatum had asked a Georgetown University colleague about that university's tuition and was startled at the $60,000-per-year tab. Even students from more affluent families who can afford Spelman's $37,000 annual price tag—students who paid at least that much at their private high schools—hope to be awarded some scholarship assistance. Those majority colleges offering black students generous scholarships had become tough rivals for bright black female students.

In essence, Tatum faced some hard decisions, and she was ready to face them head on. In recent months, she had seriously pondered taking Spelman in a dramatic new direction—one she knew would ruffle feathers. While she had not yet shared her plans with anyone beyond a close circle of insiders, Tatum was preparing to jettison the university's intercollegiate athletic program. Yes, she was ready to shut down organized sports.

The idea came upon Tatum suddenly. Spelman had been a Division III member of the NCAA since 2006. In fact, when she arrived at Spelman, the university had applied to become members, typically a four-year process. Tatum fully supported that process, believing it was a good thing to encourage young female athletes who wanted to keep playing beyond high school into college. But her thinking changed in the winter of 2011 when Spelman learned that its athletic conference, the Great South Athletic Conference, was crumbling. Trouble was, the conference needed seven members to be certified by the NCAA, yet three schools had pulled out of the conference and moved to the USA South Athletic Conference, where the football programs were more competitive.

The chaos led Tatum to conduct a bit of research on Spelman's own athletic program. What she learned surprised her: of 2,100 students at the university, only about 80 students participated in team sports, or an average of 10 to 12 students per team. The reality was that team sports were not really a significant part of Spelman's cultural fabric. On any given day, if you went to a volleyball match, or a soccer or basketball game, there were a handful of fans watching their friends play. Her concern crystallized one evening while watching a home basketball game. Earlier that day, Tatum had asked the athletic director how much Spelman was spending on its NCAA intercollegiate athletic program. The figure, $900,000, startled her. She thought, 80 students, nearly a million dollars. What a huge waste. Even more, that night as she watched the young women run up and down the court, it also hit her that those five women playing, along with the other five sitting on the bench, would likely not even touch a basketball after graduation. This was Division III, so chances were slim to none that any of them would go pro, or even play recreationally, because typically that is not what professional black women do in their spare time.

Tatum's thinking about intercollegiate sports at Spelman shifted dramatically that night. Sure, these young women loved their team sports, were passionate about athletic competition. But really, their involvement was a carryover from high school and not a predictor of their futures. What was a real predictor of their futures? Perhaps they'd leave Spelman and take up Zumba, Pilates, or yoga. Maybe they'd run 5ks, or heck, maybe they'd be sedentary—which unfortunately was the case for too many black women, younger and older. The results of sedentary habits put black women at risk for obesity, type 2 diabetes, heart disease, hypertension, and stroke.

It also occurred to Tatum that Spelman already had a strong—if underfunded—wellness program underway. Each week, some three hundred students participated. Tatum decided that instead of wasting money on the relatively fruitless intercollegiate sports program, the school should invest those dollars in Spelman's wellness program, and get some 2,100 students moving in a way that would improve their health and influence their families and communities. Yes, she thought, why not launch a wellness revolution for young black women? No, it wasn't the silver bullet idea that Spelman and so many other universities were casting about for, but this shot in the dark was certainly loud enough to make folks listen.

Women's golf at Howard University.

(Alfred Eisenstaedt/The LIFE Picture Collection/Getty Images)

CHAPTER 4

BREAK POINT

IF YOU ASK SAVANNAH BOWEN ABOUT HER
path to Howard University, she'll likely tell you about her father, a
proud Howard alum who earned his education on a tennis scholarship, or her grandfather, an immigrant from Barbados who founded
the university's cricket team in the 1950s, and how the team's photo
still hangs in Burr Gymnasium. Or she might tell you about how she
was inspired by her high school English teacher, Miss Cadet-
Simpkins, who introduced her to the works of such great black novel-
ists as Toni Morrison, whose *Beloved* changed Savannah's life.

But eventually Savannah's voice trails off, the tone of certainty in
these well-worn tales fades, and she begins to reflect and share memories of long before, back when she was five years old, when all her
friends were still asleep in the Westchester suburbs and she found
herself jogging for miles through Harlem or the South Bronx without a destination; jogging along the pathways of public parks; across
track fields and baseball diamonds, anywhere with wide open spaces.
She'll reminiscence, somewhat bitterly, about the long hours spent
under the scorching summer sun chasing tennis balls across the
court, with Coach Patrick Peters, or Coach P. C., as he was known,
standing in the distance barking a litany of orders and insults: "Shut
up and do your work!" "This is not a social club!" "You are not a
Barbie!" "Do you need some Pampers?"

It's hardly unusual among African Americans to believe that a child who grows up without some measure of mental hazing, whether it's from parents, siblings, teachers, or coaches, runs the risk of becoming an adult too soft, too unsure of themselves, to succeed in a world mostly tilted against them. A good, sustained grilling is a kind of rite of passage; born out of a belief that few success stories happen without a forceful, if not well-meaning antagonist, the sage willing to play bad cop and test the limits of strength, weakness, and patience of a developing black mind.

Coach P. C. was that guy. Full of bluster and bravado, Coach P. C., an immigrant from Ghana, was the head of the heralded Fitzpatrick Tennis Association, a program for New York City youth. There were several tennis programs for kids across the city, but Fitzpatrick was arguably the most rigorous, and Coach P. C. was the force behind the curtain; a kind of secret weapon for parents looking to prepare their children to compete against the nation's elite players. Even in memory, Savannah has mixed feelings about her time under Coach P. C., a no-nonsense disciplinarian whose tirades started the moment her parents deposited her in gritty parks in Harlem or the South Bronx and lasted until they picked her up, dead tired, at sundown. Savannah can still point to scars on her knees and elbows from falling down on a gravelly running trail her first day. She cried hard, her tragedy arousing little sympathy from her new drill sergeant. "He made it clear from the start that we were not his friends," Savannah said. "We were there to grow and work and learn how to win. It was hard core."

Infused into Coach P. C.'s teaching was a belief that black men must become more present in the lives of black youth, and that their knowledge—whether earned through triumph or failure—represents an underused asset in communities. More than ever, there should be a great urgency to prove to black kids that, despite media portrayal, black men are capable of building strong families and communities, that the black males crotch-grabbing in rap videos or being handcuffed on the evening news are hardly a fair sampling of the group. As Coach P. C. trained kids to play tennis, he made sure to weave in hard, raw truths about the effects of slavery, Jim Crow, and institutional racism on their sense of drive, character, and goals. The disappearance of black men from public school classrooms, he said, had helped to cast black men as outsiders in their own communities; Coach P. C. positioned himself as a kind of surrogate in their absence.

In Coach P. C.'s view, the narrative of their disappearance was clear. Prior to civil rights struggles, black students benefited from being taught by mostly black teachers who blended a sense of racial pride and heritage into academic lessons. Pro-black teaching had sparked, among other things, a real desire to challenge the Constitution and notions that blacks were not fully human. But with those civil rights breakthroughs came integration; the erosion of black nuclear family units due to social welfare programs that discouraged black men from living with their families; and a shakeout in public schools that ultimately pushed them out of classrooms. The result was a lost generation shaped by stereotypes of black men as disengaged at best and criminals at worst, and an overall sense that black people can't compete in mental sports. "We have to start changing this thinking in our kids," he says, "and we must start by four or five years old, because by eight or nine or ten the process is done. They already have poor diets, poor mental thinking. We have to battle with them every day, show them what to eat, how to think."

Coach P. C. tried to avoid sermonizing, instead weaving sobering racial realities and inspiration into what they saw in their everyday lives. As he watched kids scowl at the hard work he was pouring on to make them better tennis players, he would lift black male teachers on pedestals, whether it was Richard Williams, Earl Woods, or even Joe Jackson, patriarchs of superstars Venus and Serena Williams, Tiger Woods, and the Jackson entertainment dynasty, respectively.

His lessons were often less about race than about power and domination, and uncelebrated stories of black brilliance. At every opportunity, he would teach them about black achievement. While driving the van to tournaments, he might point to stoplights and remind them that the device was invented by Garrett Augustus Morgan, a black man; upon noticing one of them eating a peanut butter sandwich, he would riff on George Washington Carver; or remind them that without the inventor Frederick McKinley Jones, they would not be transporting refreshing, chilled bottles of water. When his team arrived at tournaments, generally surrounded by all-white players and audiences, Coach P. C. had a rule for them as they walked in: "Folks expect us to get out of their way," he said. "But you don't get out of anybody's way. You don't move; hold your head up and keep walking. Do not look down. You already know the floor is down there, and it ain't moving. You deserve to be here—walk like it!"

He insisted that his athletes plan big futures for themselves, which is why he discouraged them from accepting those "plum" positions as linesmen and ball boys and girls, who fetch and supply balls for players. Parents were often flabbergasted by P. C.'s rejection of such opportunities as brainwashing and re-enslavement. "Don't bring that to me; I'm not signing off on that," he'd say. "We are not here for that. We have done our service to this world as slaves. I am teaching these children that they must be the dominant ones, and accept nothing less than the dominant position." He wasn't interested in sanitizing the seriousness of his girls' mission. "I know you're only seven," he'd say matter of factly. "But repeat after me: 'I have to win.'"

Savannah was born in the Bronx, New York, but raised in more upscale nearby Westchester County, the oldest of three girls, to hardworking Caribbean parents; her father born in Washington, D.C., with roots in Barbados, and mother Haitian. Growing up, there was always an expectation, and often pressure, for Savannah and her sisters to graduate high school at the top of their class and matriculate at a top university. Part of her father's calculation was that, while a stellar classroom performance was critical, the girls needed also to become solid athletes to improve their chances of admission into the best schools. He never asked Savannah whether she wanted to play tennis; he insisted she play. "There was really no discussion, no negotiating," she said. "And I never really had gravitational pull to the sport. He just sort of put me into it."

An early family tragedy had shaped Shawn Bowen's philosophy. Born in Washington, D.C., to Marie Antoinette Collins and Bernard Keith Bowen, who met and married as Howard University undergraduates, Shawn was seven years old when his father, lighting a kerosene lamp, caught fire and nearly died after suffering first-degree burns over his entire body. His father, a Barbados native, had studied pre-med at Howard with plans to attend medical school, but was working as a taxi driver at the time of the accident. His mother, a D.C. native, fell into a deep depression, neglecting her parental duties to Shawn and his four-year-old sister, Lisa. Not yet out of grade school, Shawn was already headed in the wrong direction; hanging out with older kids in the neighborhood and getting picked up by police for such petty crimes as shoplifting and vandalism. He stayed out late into the night on street corners smoking cigarettes and looking for trouble to get into.

Shortly after his father was released from the hospital, he told his wife he was taking the children to visit family in New Jersey. This single act of deception became a turning point for Shawn. Instead of driving to New Jersey, Shawn and his baby sister wound up on a one-way flight to Barbados, where they would spend their childhood; raised in an upper-middle-class, tight-knit family of loving but fierce disciplinarians. On native soil, his father's connections ran deep, quickly securing his father work as manager at an import-export company. His reputation as an extraordinary—and dirty—soccer player preceded him. Among his friends were the country's political dignitaries and successful business people. Settling along the beach, far away from the temptations pulling him in the wrong direction in D.C., Shawn began thriving, too. In school, he proved to be a gifted student, particularly excelling in science and math. He also took up tennis, and by the time he reached his teens, he demonstrated an easy and enviable command of the sport.

Shawn was a much-changed seventeen-year-old before his feet touched American soil again. His solo trip to reconnect with family was heartbreaking. While there, along with the discovery that many of his old buddies were now dead or in prison, he learned that his mother had slipped deeply into mental illness and was homeless, living on E Street. When he found her, she was a mere shadow of the woman he recalled, and she was cold and distant toward him; the reunion was anything but what he had imagined during his decade of missing her. There were no hugs, no tears. He tried to understand their disconnect; that his father's abandonment had torn her apart.

He had overheard that their marriage was deeply troubled—and so was she—from the start. Still, it was yet another turning point for Shawn, who suddenly felt more alone and grown-up than he ever had.

He applied and was accepted into Georgetown University, but couldn't afford the tuition. Around that time, one of his aunts in Barbados passed away and willed to Shawn $2,000, enough to cover—after some financial aid and student loans—a year at Howard University, his father's alma mater.

He moved to D.C., taking up residence with his maternal grandfather, Reverend Leon Collins. His mother was suffering severe bouts of paranoia, but to an extent, he was able to become reacquainted with her. He recognized his mother, during their long walks through the city, to be a brilliant woman. She amazed him with her intricate knowledge of the city's history, geography, and plant life. He also came to appreciate the family's prominence around D.C. Reverend Collins was a graduate of Wilberforce University located in Xenia, Ohio, one of the nation's first black colleges. He presided over D.C.'s Zion Baptist Church, and had lived with his wife, Eva Mae Brown—a Xenia native who had worked at Wilberforce—in a stately home on D.C.'s upscale Gold Coast Church Row. The couple boasted close enough connections to such figures as Dr. Martin Luther King Jr. that their phone lines stayed bugged by the FBI. Shawn's maternal uncle, as it turned out, was chair of psychiatry at Howard, and a retired Army colonel.

During his freshman year at Howard, one of his tennis buddies introduced Shawn to the university's coach, Larry Strickland, who was impressed enough by Shawn's game that he offered him an athletic scholarship. It was the break Shawn was looking for. Life under his grandfather's roof was too prohibitive; there were curfews and

Shawn, who had never held a real job, had to work part-time at an auto parts warehouse to contribute to household expenses. The scholarship brought Shawn into Cook Hall, Howard's athletic dorm.

After graduating in 1988, Shawn had planned to study medicine at Howard, but a girlfriend suggested that he join her in applying to Columbia University. With Columbia's deadline approaching, he scribbled out an admissions essay, hastily dropping it in the mail, and was shocked when the university contacted him for an interview. But, by his estimation, the meeting with Columbia's admissions officer—held on a jam-packed and brutally long, so-called Black Student Day—went horribly, so much so that he chided the officer by ending the meeting with a loaded question: "I haven't met many applicants from traditionally black universities—do you find them to be insufficient?" He figured, what the heck? He was planning to attend Howard's medical school anyway.

His change of heart came after he received a letter from Howard, stating that they were aware he had applied to Columbia and essentially bemoaning how white colleges were always pillaging HBCUs for their cream of the crop. The patronizing, manipulative tone of the letter, along with what seemed an invasion of his privacy, offended Shawn. He literally struck a match and burned it. When he got a letter of acceptance from Columbia, he embraced the invitation as destiny and headed to New York. He calls it the wisest decision of his life, as that's where he would meet Magalie Balmir, his wife.

Shortly after Savannah was born, Shawn, working as a pediatrician, moved his family from the Bronx to Mount Vernon, up a few miles north to the more affluent Westchester County. The move was strategic: having grown up in Barbados, populated and governed by blacks, Shawn liked the fact that Mount Vernon boasted a black mayor in Ernie Davis—and wanted his children to see blacks in positions of authority. In fact, the mayor played tennis, and in the years to come would play socially with him and his daughters.

Savannah's mother, a New York University graduate, was a licensed practical nurse, and while the couple was hardly wealthy, they made sure to enroll their children in schools they believed could deliver a top-quality education. For grade school, Savannah attended the public Pennington-Grimes Elementary (Denzel Washington is an alum) in Mount Vernon. For middle school, her parents made the financial sacrifices to pay the tuition at The Ursuline School; a more-than-century-old private Roman Catholic all-girls K–12 academy in New Rochelle bustling with well-to-do Irish and Italian girls wearing plaid uniforms.

Savannah's daily routine was grueling: wake up at 4 a.m. and on the court by 5 a.m., and then off to school. Bedtime was 8:30 p.m. There was tennis from October through May, and in summer from June to August, pulling one another around on resistance belts to build muscle strength, and drinking gallons upon gallons of water to stay hydrated. Generally, the settings were gritty courts in the South Bronx and Harlem, where the occasional drug transaction, loud music, and rough B-boys were the norm. Occasionally, the girls were treated to better private courts such as Stadium Racquet Club, near Yankee Stadium, or Bronx International. "It was nonstop," she said. "When breaks came, I was like, 'Thank God.'"

Shawn knew that Coach P. C. was high-strung, but he appreciated his rigor, and with each tale of grunting and grinding work he felt reassured that he had picked the right mentor for his daughters.

Shawn had learned about Coach P. C. through his dentist, a fellow Howard graduate and tennis enthusiast. Coach P. C., accomplished in his own right, had traveled the world on the junior circuit playing with the best, including Arthur Ashe, who would become the only black man ever to win the singles titles at Wimbledon, the U.S. Open, and the Australian Open. After playing competitively, Coach P. C.'s mission in life turned to helping black children become professional tennis players. He had come up when tennis was even more segregated, when blacks had only one another to rely upon for instruction and inspiration. Under his tutelage, Coach P. C. wanted his charges to learn how to work hard, to invest time in something and see what black people could accomplish with some discipline and sweat. Even more, he wanted his students to appreciate their essential role in history.

His devotion to the girls bordered on fatherly. He could be wildly protective, quick to yell at any unfamiliar male who approached them: "Don't talk to this girl! You do not know her! You talk to me first if you want to talk to her!" And he was equally demanding about his girls' expectations of themselves. "I don't want to see anybody becoming anybody's ball boy," he would say. "People will be getting balls for you." To him, success was a mind job; he did not want his pupils to even imagine a life in servitude. He wanted them to build an identity through the eyes of a boss, not a servant.

In Coach P. C., Shawn knew he had found the perfect foil for Savannah. Left on her own, Savannah would have found contentment in becoming a bookworm. Unlike her younger sister, Averie, who was gifted and driven athletically, Savannah was not interested in running or exerting herself physically. But even Shawn found himself wincing at how hard Coach P. C. pushed them, these little girls running ten miles per day; a few parents even threatened to call child services on him. Shawn knew that Savannah would quit tennis eventually, but he didn't want her to fear the idea of pushing herself to her limits. He certainly didn't want to scar her psychologically, though, and he prayed that Savannah wouldn't grow to resent him.

At Ursuline, Savannah was emerging as a star, plucked in the seventh grade to play on the varsity team. And at Fitzpatrick, Coach P. C. had put her under the tutelage of her first female coach, Coach Monique, an artsy white New Zealander married to a black man in Harlem. Her game improved immeasurably under Coach Monique's mild-mannered instruction. It didn't hurt that Savannah enjoyed a growth spurt that not only added even more reach to her lanky frame; it also dramatically bolstered her speed and agility.

Meanwhile, she was discovering there was actually a method to Coach P. C.'s madness, that what seemed at times an ego-driven obsession with creating young tennis champions was actually a deeper desire for them to succeed in a world largely divided by race. To him, tennis could unlock the most important lessons in life.

She still remembers the afternoon Coach P. C. commanded his girls to line up so that he could teach them how to walk. The team chuckled and rolled their eyes at their coach's odd request. Annoyed, Coach P. C. demonstrated what he meant; how to really walk properly, head upright, shoulders back, one foot striding in front of the other in a confident gait. This was serious stuff to him. He told them that they were competing in a sport that was traditionally white, and that they were representing their race every time they stepped onto the court.

That afternoon, Coach P. C. watched and critiqued each of the girls as they walked before him, and ended the lesson with another of his favorite phrases: "That's what you do after busting some white boy's ass."

By tenth grade, Savannah had transferred to Pelham Memorial High School, the town's only public high school that boasts a decidedly small affluent student body—850 students—and a 94 percent graduation rate. Savannah had begun to sense that her black identity differed slightly, yet significantly, from her tight network of African American friends. In ways subtle and blatant, the white kids at school often perpetuated a myth of their own superiority. Black kids were mostly viewed negatively, and with suspicion. For Savannah, the racial divide was troubling; surrounded by adoring white friends impressed by her academic prowess and feats on the tennis court, Savannah could almost feel their cool judgment whenever they observed her chatting with black kids. There was this one streetwise black guy who routinely flirted with Savannah, and while she held no romantic interest in him, she found him to be nice enough for simple small talk. But her white friends attacked the budding friendship, warning her that he was a bad person whom she should avoid. She would later regret bowing to such peer pressure.

While the stigma attached to blackness cast a pall on her experiences, Savannah knew better than to take it to heart. Her parents, unabashedly proud of their Caribbean roots, seemed generally unaffected by how white Americans viewed them. "My parents were never like, 'we are Caribbean people, and not like African Americans,'" she said. "But the culture of my household . . . everyone is getting an education. We were pushed into these predominantly white schools, and it was 'You are not like these white girls; you have to work hard, be twice as good, and not act up.'"

Savannah's self-esteem was anchored, meanwhile, in stories her father told of life back in Barbados, where the prime minister was black and whites were the minority; or her mother, who, with her sisters, arrived from Haiti as young girls not speaking a word of English, and all put themselves through college. The underlying message: "It's not inherent in this nation to consider that black is equal, and that psyche is something we have to break out of," she said. "If you come here with nothing, and you have to work hard to survive, it gives you a certain drive that is different than the African American struggle."

It was at Pelham Memorial High that Savannah, who had a stubborn streak, started resenting being forced to play tennis, and protested as much to her father. In her junior year, she quit the team and ran cross-country instead. Disappointed in her decision, but with Savannah having evolved into a strong-willed young woman from a docile little girl, he could only reiterate his view on the matter: "Look, I can't afford to send three of you to college. You all will have to find a way to do that for yourself. I know you love school and you're academically driven, but I want you to have it all—academic and athletic. Believe me, your tennis will make you a stronger applicant. It will open doors; you'll meet people who will become valuable in your life."

During her senior year, Savannah did, in fact, meet someone valuable who would open doors for her—but it wasn't on the tennis court. It was in a small, brightly lit classroom tucked away on the second floor of Pelham Memorial High. That's where she met Miss Valerie Cadet-Simpkins, her new English teacher.

Morgan State University students *(from left to right)* Michael Osikomaiya, Craig Cornish, and Kyle De Jan celebrate winning $50,000 in grant money for their school at the Honda Campus All-Star Challenge at the automaker's headquarters in Torrance, California.

(Eric Reed/AP for Honda American Motor Co., Inc.)

CHAPTER 5

LETTER FROM A TRUSTEE

THROUGH THE YEARS, RENEE HIGGINBOTHAM-Brooks had earned a reputation as an unflappable leader, the sort who could sit coolly through the worst of drubbings without a hint of anger or remorse. Yet she admitted that as she hung up the phone during that April morning, her hands were trembling and tears were in her eyes. She had just spent a few minutes on the phone with Barry Rand, the chair of Howard University's board of trustees, the one man in the world who knew how to get under her skin. "That was the very worst conversation I have ever had with a man in all my life," she said.

Despite her diminutive stature, Higginbotham-Brooks has always relished a good scrap with men, especially the arrogant ones. She had battled more than her share—in courtrooms, boardrooms, and in her personal life. She had learned early on that women who were afraid to confront men got nowhere in life, no matter how pretty or talented they were. She had taught as much to her two daughters, Leigh and Codie, and thus far was proud those lessons had taken hold.

Of course, when she talks about that other brute that once entered her life, cancer, her tone softens considerably. The topic cuts quickly to the human part of Higginbotham-Brooks, the fragility of the overworked single mother she had successfully hidden from colleagues in the court and the boardroom. Looking back, the entire episode seems surreal to her now: how, in the spring of 2002, she awoke in the middle of the night and knew something was wrong. "It was just a voice," she said. "I went to the doctor and he told me that I have a growth in my breast and they need to biopsy it."

The diagnosis was breast cancer, first stage. "The doctor said, 'Look, you gotta get this taken care of right now, Renee. You don't know about cancer. Cancer cells will jump all over in your body.'" She weighed her options. With a mastectomy, she could avoid chemotherapy and radiation. If they did a lumpectomy, she would still have to have at least radiation. She told him she didn't want any of that chemo or radiation stuff. Then have it all removed, the doctor said.

Without that decision, Higginbotham-Brooks was already under enough stress; her law practice was thriving, but had also become a beast to control; from managing her firm's hundreds of municipal cases across the state, to endless travel across the country for clients wanting access to mayors. On top of it all, she had three properties: a home in Fort Worth, a weekend condo on ritzy Fisher Island in Florida, and the condo at the Ritz-Carlton hotel in Washington, D.C. But she refused to think the worst; she had detected the cancer early and could now seek the best treatment.

Higginbotham-Brooks opted for a double mastectomy with reconstruction. But instead of undergoing surgery at home in Fort Worth, she sought the expertise of the only institution she truly trusted: Howard University. Taking a few months off, she moved temporarily to D.C. and became a patient of Dr. LaSalle Leffall Jr., chief of surgery at Howard University Hospital. She knew she was in good hands. Since Howard's founding only three individuals had occupied the position of chief of surgery, the legendary Charles Drew, Burke "Mickey" Syphax, and LaSalle Leffall. Even more than the university's president, the role was arguably the most important

at Howard. The seventy-three-year-old Leffall, whose affable de-
meanor and quick laugh belied his gifts as a surgeon and a remarkable résumé that included chairman of Susan G. Komen and
president of the American Cancer Society. "Renee, after you finish
your treatment and you leave here, my goal is to have you cancer free
and for you to look just like you look now," Leffall told her.

After her surgery, Higginbotham-Brooks spent the next six weeks
at the Ritz-Carlton recovering in a kind of mental haze, sore and
drained of energy. Satisfied by her progress, Dr. Leffall extracted
tissue from her lymph nodes and ran several tests to determine the
risk factors of reoccurrence. His report back to her made her weep
with relief. "Renee, I have been practicing medicine for fifty years,
and I have never had a patient in which I see none of the risk factors
related to reoccurrence." He took her hand. "I pronounce you cured."

Incidentally, one of her good friends was a producer for *The
Oprah Winfrey Show*, and invited Higginbotham-Brooks to share
her story on a segment focusing on breast cancer. She was hesitant
initially, but agreed after they offered to come tape her at her
home. The crew showed up on a Sunday, and spent the day with
Higginbotham-Brooks and her daughters, dredging up all sorts of
drama and emotion. Actually, it was more fun than she imagined,
especially being flown later to Chicago to talk to Oprah live in the
Harpo studio. She was inspired to meet other courageous women in
the audience who had battled cancer and were still alive to talk
about it.

The crisis had toughened Higginbotham-Brooks, and she had
sensed a fight with Rand coming for quite some time. Even as proof

piled up that Ribeau's tenure as president of Howard University was disastrous, Rand had remained a staunch loyalist, an apologist really. Sure, there were cosmetic signs of progress, such as two new dormitories being built on campus to the tune of $107 million. But in reality, Howard was hemorrhaging cash, thanks to plummeting student enrollment that fall semester—some four hundred students didn't return for classes—along with various other revenue shortfalls and a pending cash drain due to Howard's federal appropriation decrease caused by sequestration. As Ribeau announced to staff in an internal memo: "In spite of the contingency funding, we will not be able to balance the operational budget without implementing major cost-saving initiatives over the final two quarters of the fiscal year."

Higginbotham-Brooks and Rand feigned civility in public, but their relationship behind the scenes was salty. The rift dated all the way back to the search process for Patrick Swygert's successor—which, in Higginbotham-Brooks's view, was shady at best. Rand was on the search committee, and the running had narrowed to two candidates, Ribeau and Ronald Mason, then president of Jackson State. Higginbotham-Brooks preferred Mason, as he had been a guest in her home back in Fort Worth a few years back when she and Bill Cosby hosted a dialogue about the crisis among black males. Such meetings were therapeutic for Cosby, whose son, Ennis, was murdered in 1997 during an attempted robbery—and Cosby seemed captivated by Mason's insights on the hampered progress of African American males.

Higginbotham-Brooks recalled Rand taking her aside and admitting to her that Ribeau was the brother of his ex-wife, Jane. But he downplayed the connection, saying he had married Jane in his early twenties and that Ribeau was a young boy then and that he had little contact with him. He conceded, though, that he and his ex had remained close friends through the years.

Higginbotham-Brooks's legal instincts kicked in. She told Rand in no uncertain terms that he needed to disclose this fact to the Howard community, that it would look really bad if this prior relationship got out. Rand assured Higginbotham-Brooks that he would and, according to the letter to the *Washington Post* from search committee cochairs Richard Parsons and Colin Powell, he did.

The boiling point came the morning at the Fairmont Hotel when Higginbotham-Brooks overheard Rand's backroom compensation discussion with Ribeau and confronted Rand afterward. She told him that the conversation made her quite uncomfortable. He explained that he had the authority of the compensation committee to talk to him about his contract. Higginbotham-Brooks said she didn't care whose authority he had; he should have had somebody else in this room. The perception was bad, she said, from a legal perspective. "I would have never let a client do what he did. Never," she said. "He should have had the general counsel there, or anyone other than merely himself. That whole deal would never pass anyone's smell test." In response to Higginbotham-Brooks's version of events, current trustee chair Stacey Mobley insists that Ribeau's compensation contract was negotiated by the board's compensation committee and that any assumption otherwise is inaccurate. Rand declined to comment on Higginbotham-Brooks's account of their exchange.

That's where the beef started, and it continued over the next couple of years with Rand, in her eyes, excluding Higginbotham-Brooks from the board's decision-making process whenever he could because she knew too much. She now kicked herself for not raising a red flag to the board, reasoning back then that despite Ribeau's slick entry he might just make a good president. After all, during interviews he was remarkably prepared, rattling off the right responses to the tough questions hurled at him. Of course, she now speculated—after Ribeau's continuous flubbing on the job—that Rand had thoroughly prepped his former brother-in-law for those interviews.

With Ribeau's contract up for renewal, Higginbotham-Brooks had begun lobbying the trustees behind the scenes to consider a leadership change. She pressed them about how the university was going down the tubes, in her mind, due in part to Ribeau handing the university's reins over to a contracted CFO—Robert M. Tarola, a white guy whose small firm was raking in north of a million and who rarely interacted with other staff. This CFO was not only making tons of money, he was controlling everybody; from facilities to construction to administrators' salaries. Adding insult to injury, there were reasons to doubt his affinity for black colleges generally. It was rumored that during his private meetings with other white colleagues in the finance world, he'd boast that if it weren't for his expertise Howard would be closed today. Once during a bond transaction meeting, an administrator and Howard alum overheard him saying to a group of white underwriters, "Who needs HBCUs anyway? I don't understand what it is about these HBCUs."

Granted, many of Higginbotham-Brooks's gripes about Tarola were less about his job performance than his tenuous connection to the university. Still, she blamed the enrollment drop on the CFO's decision to build his budget on 10,500 students without consulting the academic side for a count of how many students were actually coming to school that fall. And nobody was even discussing the sequestration, let alone figuring out a way to balance the hospital's financial interests with its mission to provide health services to the indigent.

There were the deeper issues, too. Among them: Howard had 5,000 employees on its payroll to educate only 10,000 students. These numbers didn't include the hospital, which employed another 1,671 people. "What was Howard running, a university or a jobs program?" Higginbotham-Brooks liked to ask. The personnel bloat only heightened outrage over students being forced to leave the university because they didn't have another $3,000 or $5,000 to stay and graduate.

"And you've got this consulting firm pulling down 1.6 million dollars and its CFO Tarola, just having a good old time working in a secured area where you weren't granted access unless you've been cleared and buzzed in," Higginbotham-Brooks went on. "Not even with the rest of the black folks in the administration building, but with his folks in a different building. And running the school! He was telling the academic side and the operations side, you're over budget and I'm not approving this or that."

Sure, things could have been bad under any leader Howard had selected. But Higginbotham-Brooks was pissed off because she knew the conniving story about how Ribeau had gotten there, and how the school had suffered the past five years with him at the helm, suffering she believed would have been avoided with Mason as president.

Ribeau and Tarola have denied accusations of mismanagement, but in support of Higginbotham-Brooks's view, the university's accounting firm, PricewaterhouseCoopers, broke ties, saying the firm lacked confidence in the university's management and its financial controls. They had come on under Ribeau and would request financial information but rarely receive anything they needed for a proper audit. One of the firm's partners, a Howard graduate, had tears in his eyes as he broke the news. He was apologetic and said that he tried his best to talk his partners into staying on, but the books and processes were just too messy.

Amid Higginbotham-Brooks's expressing her disapproval to fellow trustees about Howard's weakening state, the board decided to split her vice chair duties with Benaree Pratt Wiley—a Howard alum and corporate management consultant—without even notifying her. She learned of the change during a regular board meeting. There was no doubt in her mind that the change—possibly a breach of the bylaws, Higginbotham-Brooks says—was the work of Barry Rand. Outraged and embarrassed by the dilution of her role, Higginbotham-Brooks called Rand several times the following day but failed to reach him. Finally, she left a message on Rand's answering machine.

"Barry Rand, this is Renee Brooks. I didn't appreciate what happened in the board meeting and I know you understand why. You need to have Benny back off and you need to restore it to the way it was. And if I don't hear from you in twenty-four hours, I am going to call for a vote of no-confidence in the chairman and the president. But I'm really trying to tell you to call me back. Call me back, please. I just need to talk to you."

According to Higginbotham-Brooks, the following morning, Rand called her back. In her recollection of the exchange, he was clearly upset.

"Yes, Renee, I got your message, and what are you doing trying to threaten me?"

"I'm not trying to threaten you."

"Oh, yes you are."

"Barry, you know and I know you don't return phone calls. And if you do it's weeks later. If I didn't say something like that, you weren't going to call me back. And I needed to talk to you because you know that was wrong."

"Wrong? What do you mean wrong? Why does it have to be *wrong*. Nobody has to talk to you first. Who has to talk to you? Why?"

"Well, Barry, that's common sense. That's normal courtesy. There should be some explanation for what you did."

"What do you mean, *I did?* Why do you think I'm *doing* stuff?"

"Barry, you know and I know that couldn't have happened without you knowing about it."

"Of course I knew about it, but I didn't plan it."

"Okay, Barry."

"But you threatened me. And you have no right to threaten me."

"What do you mean threaten you?"

"You called me on the phone, and said that if I didn't do something in twenty-four hours, you were going to call for a vote of no-confidence. That was a threat—and I don't take threats lightly! How dare you!"

"Barry, that's not the case."

"Oh, yes it is."

Rand went on for a while about the threat, and then moved on.

"First of all, who cares what you think. You may have friends on the board but nobody respects you. And quite honestly, if you were a man . . ."

"Let's talk about Howard, let's talk about what's in the best interest of Howard. Let's put this mess behind us."

"You're just trying to sweet talk me, with your sweet little words.

That's what you're trying to do. Trying to turn what I say around. You're a lawyer. All you want to do is put words in my mouth."

"Let's put away all our disagreements and focus on what needs to be done. Because a lot needs to be done. . . ." Higginbotham-Brooks repeated this several times but to no avail, as Rand focused again on her apparent threat to him.

"If you were a man, I'd be up in your face!"

His temper continued to escalate. "You have no right to threaten me. Your behavior needs to be known by the board. It is disgusting, threatening me. How dare you. Nobody threatens me. Nobody has the balls to threaten me. Not even the president of the United States. Because I am Barry Rand."

"Really." Higginbotham-Brooks was dumbfounded.

"And listen, if you get out of line again, I'm going to play that tape. Because I got it on tape. I got your threats on tape."

"Really, Barry, I am not threatening you."

"Oh, yes you are."

"Okay that's enough. I've heard enough. I understand. Good-bye."

Rand has not commented on Higginbotham-Brooks's version of events. But Higginbotham-Brooks says that when she hung up the phone, she was in tears. She had never been talked down to in such a way in her life. She was hurt, angry, and outraged all at once. She called a couple of close board colleagues and talked about—and was quickly talked out of—resigning her board seat. Then she got on the phone and strategized with a longtime classmate and confidante. They decided the best course of action was for Higginbotham-Brooks to outline her concerns to the board in a formal letter, and spent a few hours writing the letter.

Higginbotham-Brooks had her assistant call the secretary of the board's office to figure out how to submit her letter to what she thought was the board's secure electronic portal.

That process turned out to be trickier than she expected. Higginbotham-Brooks's secretary tried calling the board secretary several times, but couldn't reach her. She said she was traveling during this period of time. Finally, Higginbotham-Brooks's office contacted someone on the board's support staff, and she was walked through the process of posting the letter on the portal.

A few hours after posting the letter, Higginbotham-Brooks received a call from the secretary of the board, who has a law degree. "That portal is not secure."

"I thought the portal was secure."

"Girl, anybody can go on that portal and not only look at stuff but can pull it off. There's no telling where that letter is going to end up."

Renee Higginbotham-Brooks's letter was posted on the trustees' portal on April 24.

Dear Fellow Trustees:

It is with a heavy heart that I write to you to share my disappointment with the outcome of our most recent Board meeting.

As a Howard Alumna and a member of this Board for the past 14 years, I have served as Vice Chair since 2005. I have donated over $350,000 to the University and personally raised another $500,000 and I believe my contributions, love and devotion to our university are beyond reproach.

I can no longer sit quietly, notwithstanding my personal preference to avoid confrontation, and therefore, I am compelled to step forward to announce that our beloved University is in genuine trouble and "time is of the essence."

Howard will not be here in three years if we don't make some crucial decisions now.

- The combination of fewer students who can arrange financial aid, coupled with high school counselors who are steering students to less expensive state and junior colleges, has resulted in lower enrollment and this trend is expected to continue.

- Howard's Federal appropriation is expected to be decreased because of sequestration and the rationale for the University's existence is expected to be challenged since African American students can attend any college or university today.

- The Hospital has become a serious drain on the budget of the University and we need to either sell it or get the D.C. government to properly reimburse us for the care provided to its citizens.

- We lack an infrastructure for fundraising to replace decreasing tuition revenue and shrinking Federal dollars, and we lack access to the larger philanthropic community.

- We have too many employees on our payroll (approximately 5,000 employees to serve less than 10,000 students) and we cannot afford this!

We have ignored one impropriety after another beginning with the personal relationship between the President and the Chairman. After five years, we know their partnership has not served us well. In addition, the President's lackluster job performance has resulted in many poor decisions in finance, staffing, operations and internal and external communications and that poor performance has drained the University of its funds, students, faculty and alumni support, and it has damaged our University's brand.

What occurred at the last Board meeting was only a symptom of the larger problems we must finally confront. Notwithstanding our ongoing conversations and concern about the direction and leadership of our beloved Alma Mater, our Board has not taken any action to improve its leadership or to address our concerns. Instead, we voted to marginalize the position of Vice Chair of the Board of Trustees and me. I was never consulted or advised of the bifurcation of my position as Vice Chair until one minute before I walked into the boardroom on Saturday. I was shocked, truly offended, and extremely disappointed with this underhanded tactic, which is inconsistent with the manner in which we do business as a Board.

This significant change in our governance structure altered a position—that of Vice Chair—that has been in place for the past 30+ years and the fact that this change was accomplished without any discussion with me or the Executive Committee, and without any vote of the full Board, suggests that this Chairman believes he can operate as though the University is his own personal corporation. We, as the Board, must insist that democratic processes are at the foundation of our governance.

We need to convene an emergency meeting to discuss the dysfunctional environment that is so pervasive throughout the University and the prevalent improprieties that plague its administration, and to begin a process of formulating a plan to address the very serious problems that exist today.

I suggest we immediately convene a confidential meeting during which we can discuss the detailed specifics of what has occurred on our watch, and determine how we will meet our fiduciary duty to the Howard community going forward. Therefore, I am hereby calling for an immediate and emergency meeting of the Board of Trustees to consider a vote of no confidence in both the Chairman of the Board and the President, and I insist that this meeting occur before any new members are added to our Board. This is not something they should have to confront upon their arrival to serve the University.

The future of this University is at stake and there comes a time when each of us will have to stand for what is right and just. I hope you will stand with me now.

Sincerely,
Renee Higginbotham-Brooks

Morehouse College student Philip Maundu,
a native Kenyan, stands under a racially discriminate
real estate sign.

(Ted Russell/The LIFE Picture Collection)

CHAPTER 6

THE NEW BLACK ON BLACK CRIME

WHEN UMUHIRE LILIANE NTABANA (SHE GOES by Liliane) was seven years old, Hutu soldiers stormed her home in Rwanda, during a massacre that claimed the lives of some eight hundred thousand men, women, and children in the Tutsi minority.

By God's grace, Liliane's life was spared. One of the Hutu soldiers, his boot pinning her down, had mercy on her. "You look like my daughter," she recalled him saying. "So I'm not going to kill you. But we will have to kill the others." The slaughter that night included her father, mother, three sisters, and several aunts and uncles. She has two brothers and two sisters who survived (and another brother who is missing), spread out across Canada, England, India, and Sweden.

Liliane is still traumatized by the memory of visiting her aunt at a hospital in Kigali. As though yesterday, she vividly recalls the stench of patients suffering from cancer, HIV, and other diseases packed like sardines into airless single rooms. Among them was her beautiful aunt, who had been raped during the genocide and was infected with HIV, who lay hungry in a twin bed with an ailing bedmate. The experience again brought into stark relief the importance of good affordable health care, and spurred her desire to help folks in need.

The HBCU student (first generation, African American) must now compete against a new crop of talented internationals, thanks to the recent wave of students arriving from such countries as Haiti, South Africa, and Jamaica, and bringing with them their own survivor narratives. Their foreign tales of hardship and perseverance often make their African American peers look like slackers by comparison. The courting of foreign students, and the millions of dollars in scholarships that comes with them, is a touchy topic these days at HBCUs. On one hand, as black colleges struggle to improve retention and graduation rates, tapping a new, talented pool of high-achieving internationals offers a quick boost to the university's overall academic performance. Yet recruiting overseas also represents a clear break in the traditional mission of HBCUs.

At Johnson C. Smith University, you'd be hard-pressed to find a student with more drive or harrowing a story than Liliane. She's hardworking, bashful with a razor-sharp wit. Yet she has forged tight bonds with students at Johnson C. Smith University whose biographies and interests are decidedly different from her own, their main commonality being that JCSU has proven both safety net and catalyst. In the rancor surrounding black colleges these days, you don't hear much about the Lilianes—the talk is mostly about poor faculty pay, federal-funding cuts, deteriorating facilities, and ambitious capital campaigns. You don't hear much about the students like Liliane, who crystallize much of the hope—and at times, doubt—surrounding today's black colleges.

The youngest of nine children, Liliane plans to one day become a dentist like her late father. She can tell you the exact moment her ambition was sparked: she was five years old, at home in her native Kigali, Rwanda, and a man arrived crying with pain from a toothache. Her father spirited the man to the clinic and treated him, and Liliane recalls the man coming back to the house again smiling with gratitude. What an awesome and rewarding way to help your fellow man, Liliane thought.

In 2008, after testifying against a Hutu soldier involved in the killings, Liliane fled Rwanda for Boston, applied for asylum, and worked a series of odd jobs, including attending parking lots and cleaning up restaurants, hotel rooms, and airplane cabins. She took classes at Bunker Hill Community College, and worked hard on her English. She also met another Rwandan family who connected her to Dr. Ron Carter, the president of Johnson C. Smith University. Touched by Liliane's trials and perseverance, Carter offered her a scholarship for international students funded by the university's Duke endowment. Liliane graduated in 2014 with a degree in biology, and plans to attend dental school at the University of North Carolina at Chapel Hill. If you ask Liliane what she likes to do in her spare time, her answer is quick and resolute: "I pray," she says. "That's what I do."

Among Liliane's friends is Radijah Hudson, whose earlier path in life seemed headed anywhere but college. Her mother was eighteen, a girl herself, when she gave birth to Radijah in 1993, in Baton Rouge, Louisiana. When Radijah was born, her father had just begun a fifteen-year sentence in prison for armed robbery. One of her earliest memories is visiting him in the penitentiary, and her mother forcing her to take a picture with the stranger. For the first seven years of her life, Radijah was raised by her maternal great-grandmother, the family's wise and tough-loving matriarch who, between cooking the best meals ever, told scary stories about ghosts and voodoo to the grandkids. The men in her family existed mostly on the margins of Radijah's life; she had heard about how her great-grandfather, nicknamed Daddy Apple Hudson, was born with the surname Hutchison, but couldn't spell it and starting signing Hudson instead. There wasn't much of an emphasis on formal schooling in her family. Her mother did earn an associate's degree, and one of her uncles was a certified electrician. Most, though, like her great-grandmother, made it only as far as eighth grade, while others rose no further than high school.

As far back as she can remember, Radijah loved school—and it came fairly easily to her, especially math. As a student at Shenandoah Elementary, the mostly white school where she was bussed, and later all-black Wedgewood Elementary, her favorite subject was math. Her proficiency was impressive enough that in third grade, Shenandoah skipped her ahead to the fourth-grade level. She loved reading, too, but mastering the subject came less easily to her. She attributes her early reading struggles with being prematurely promoted into a gifted reading program, and losing her confidence.

When Radijah was in sixth grade, her mother moved her and her younger brother to Atlanta. Times were hard financially, with her mother only sporadically working odd jobs. By her count, from Radijah's years in junior high through high school, her family was evicted from various apartments some seven times. She was a student at Creekside High School when she took an interest in modern dance and proved gifted during competitions and performances throughout the region. During her senior year, she entered a competition at Johnson C. Smith University, and her routine earned her a performing arts scholarship to the university.

Currently a college junior, Radijah has entrepreneurial aspirations. She hopes to one day start her own dance studio, and has developed and pitched her business plan in Queen City Forward, a nonprofit business incubator. Her fallback plan is getting her teaching certificate to teach high school math. With her future sights set high, returning home to Atlanta admittedly can be tough. "It's always the same mindset, the same hurdles," she said. "Money problems, eviction notices, bills, transportation issues, anything that deals with money is a problem." During a recent Christmas holiday, her mother, facing another eviction, asked to borrow money that Radijah had saved from various part-time jobs. Radijah pushed back on the loan. "I love my family, but going home just puts fire under my ass to do what I gotta do in life," she said. "It's hard, but I love what college has done for me, and the person I'm becoming."

One of Radijah's friends is Kyle, who recently graduated from JCSU. Kyle is an easy guy to like. He has a ready smile, a warm disposition, and a solid handshake. He also boasts plenty of what his colleagues called "swag"—that surplus of quiet confidence and charisma from which good fortune tends to grow. He is tall and regal, with the dark, chiseled features of a Zulu warrior, yet dressed in polo shirts, khakis, and argyle socks. It was a powerful contrast—a kind of brutish-intellectual thing. On a campus populated by kids drowning in urban gear (oversized hoodies, saggy jeans, door-knocker earrings), Kyle stood out as serious and wise beyond his years.

At a small university like JCSU, faculty wears many hats. Among my roles was to create and supervise an entrepreneurial leadership program, and Kyle, at first blush, seemed perfect for the program. Asking around a bit, there was more reassurance about his promise: from the time Kyle's penny loafers left Alabama and touched Johnson C. Smith University's campus, he had amassed an enviable network of friends, along with a host of doting faculty

111

and administrators. Now a senior, Kyle reigned as a kind of de facto Class King, the university standard-bearer, the dashing business major trotted out during orientations to woo the parents of new recruits and corporate donors with his neat haircut and good enunciation.

Later that week, Kyle was invited to join the program and even meet with one of the city's most successful technology entrepreneurs and venture capitalists. It was impressive that Kyle had brought with him a solid business idea to the meeting, plans for a money management app for students. Kyle and the entrepreneur, a middle-aged white guy, hit it off splendidly. Not only did he offer to help Kyle write a business plan for the app, he also talked about the possibility of funding a prototype for an upcoming national college business pitch competition.

But during the car ride back to campus, as we pulled away from shiny uptown Charlotte, along the darkening gritty streets surrounding the university, something hit me: the national business pitch competition required a 3.5 grade point average. That seemed pretty high to me, but Kyle's must have been strong, considering his impressive profile among university brass.

Still, driving along, there was a sudden inclination to ask Kyle before we got too far into the process. "So, how you doing in school?"

His reply was slow. I decided not to be alarmed. Let him take his time, clear his throat, and hit me, wham, with the big number. But there was nothing. Not a sound issued. Finally, after a long pause, he mumbled: "Not so good."

"What's your GPA?"

This time, there was a longer delay. And then finally the response came.

"Two point nine," Kyle said. "I attribute that to a bad freshman year."

By now, we were a couple of miles from the downtown business incubator and Charlotte's glittery skyline was fully in my rearview. Turning into campus, it was hard not to feel crestfallen. There was also breaking the news to Kyle, this bright, ambitious young man, that he wasn't qualified to present his business idea against students from other colleges nationally. Sitting there behind the wheel, I could almost hear the cartoon score, the womp-womp-womp of my own failure. I shook Kyle's hand, trying to hide how deflated I was. As he got out of the car, I watched him stride confidently toward his dormitory. And I wondered, guiltily, how it turned out that one of our university's brightest stars dimmed once outside our gates.

Dressed casually in sweatpants and sneakers, Johnny Taylor, the blunt-talking president and CEO of the nonprofit Thurgood Marshall College Fund, was lounging at home one spring afternoon holding court about how so many black college leaders were cheating students these days; how they sermonized about offering a top-notch education while delivering subpar instruction and degrees of questionable value; how they liked to publicly demonize wealthy white Republicans while quietly courting them for funding despite, in many cases, their harmful social agendas; how they pushed for and pocketed hefty salaries, all the while cutting back on crucial staff and resources, and refused to make basic business decisions that could lead to operational efficiencies and savings.

The whole scenario was a travesty, he insisted, not only because it shortchanged students, but because the practices were unsustainable over the long haul. Few within the black college community wanted to admit it, Taylor went on to say, but that old reputation of black college excellence—a nostalgia born during the days of racial segregation—wasn't so true anymore, not at most black colleges. Even the best, while strong, were not what they used to be. "The fact of the matter is that the profile of the entering class at Howard can't even be compared to the entering class at Howard thirty years ago," he said.

Young, good-looking, and razor-smart, Johnny Taylor was fast gaining a reputation as a fearless and straight shooter, and one of the most powerful players in the HBCU community. The Thurgood Marshall College Fund (TMCF), founded in 1987, supports forty-seven schools, including public historically black colleges and medical and law schools, or some three hundred thousand students. By the spring of 2013, Taylor was going full throttle in tough love advocacy for HBCUs. He was particularly critical of the Obama administration, even threatening to sue it for its new federal financial aid policies that disproportionately affected students at majority black institutions. "We're going to continue to pursue the legislative process to find a better solution," he told a *Washington Times* reporter. "If at some point we determine that there is no agreement, then we may have to consider going to the courts."

Johnny Taylor, if anything, was gutsy. The first time I met him was in 2006 in Charlotte, North Carolina, where we both lived and where he launched an Internet search engine tailored to black audiences. A protégé of business magnate Barry Diller, the former head of such media giants as Paramount Pictures and 21st Century Fox Inc., Taylor, an attorney, had previously served as a top human resources executive for Diller's IAC/InterActiveCorp. Diller, hoping to cash in on the then-booming search engine market, had encouraged Taylor to launch the search engine, called RushmoreDrive .com. But when Diller decided to start divesting assets, and spin off a number of his businesses, Taylor got cold feet and decided to move on. Around that time, the Thurgood Marshall College Fund, where Taylor served on the board, was looking for new leadership. The organization's board chair, NBA commissioner David Stern, asked Taylor to take on the role, and Taylor, looking for a new opportunity, welcomed the challenge of remaking himself in the world of nonprofits.

As head of the nearly thirty-year-old organization, Taylor embodied a growing cadre of realists and critics finally willing to talk truth about the dire circumstances and contradictions surrounding HBCUs; the funding gap, the performance issues, the cultural and class issues that permeate black higher education. Much of Taylor's fearlessness can be attributed to his lack of deep allegiances and loyalties within the HBCU community. For example, he didn't attend an HBCU; he attended Drake University for law school and the University of Miami for undergraduate. He had become closely acquainted with HBCUs as the kingpin Barry Diller's philanthropic liaison to important black causes. In other words, he showed up at the black table carrying Diller's checkbook.

Taylor believed most HBCU leaders were asleep at the wheel, wrongly viewing their competitive crisis as merely another typical bump in the road. The reality was that HBCUs were suffering as they never had before; he was quick to rattle off facts: in a three-year span, access to summer Pell grants was eliminated, Pell grant eligibility was reduced to twelve semesters, Title III (B) funding was cut due to sequestration, and the Obama administration had unilaterally tightened the credit limits for families relying on loans to fund their children's education. All of this while the black community dealt with chronically stubborn unemployment—double that of white Americans—in the wake of the Great Recession. Perhaps most significantly, he chastised HBCUs for not holding up their own end of the bargain. "We as a community have got to own that some of our problems, many of our problems, are of our own making and we continue to perpetuate them," he often said.

Taylor was fierce because he himself was born into and overcame some steep hurdles. He barely knew his father; he and his three siblings were raised by a single mother in the tough section of Fort Lauderdale, Florida. Fortunately he was a strong student and earned scholarships to the University of Miami before going on to law school at Drake. During his rise at IAC, he sat on several boards and was always involved, pushing his employers to support black schools—despite the fact that, ironically, he was not recruited by any. "I have always written big checks, consistently," he said. Through his own testimony, he came to believe one thing: education is the great equalizer. There was no better place to trumpet that message, he figured, than the Thurgood Marshall College Fund. "It is my calling," he said.

Taylor's honeymoon in the black college community was short-lived. For many, his pedigree—his education at predominately white institutions, lack of a Ph.D., and rise under a white billionaire—simply struck a wrong note, as though flourishing among high-powered whites automatically rendered him suspect. Shortly after he took office he gave several speeches at black colleges and afterward would invariably be peppered with barbed questions by faculty and administrators. He recalled one instance in particular when a professor raised her hand and went on to challenge his thinking on the future of HBCUs, strongly suggesting that his not attending an HBCU strained his credibility on the issue. Taylor was respectful, but calmly explained that while he didn't attend a black college, his life was heavily influenced by them. "I'm a product of the HBCUs," he told her. "All of the teachers in Fort Lauderdale were HBCU graduates; my doctors, my lawyers, everybody I knew was an HBCU graduate. Everything I am is because of HBCUs." Then he said: "I'm also the guy who just wrote a hundred-thousand-dollar check to HBCUs. How much have you given?" The room was silent.

Taylor's rationale was both simple and compelling: some fifty years ago, if you were a college student, you attended a black college. As late at the mid-1970s, for example, some 35 percent of blacks attended an HBCU, according to the U.S. Department of Education. One of the by-products of racial segregation was that black colleges enjoyed a critical mass of really smart students, and really bright teachers whose options were also limited. Along with great students and faculty, the black community placed a high value on education and backed it by giving to schools, especially the churches.

But integration changed all that, as white universities began admitting talented black students who before had enjoyed few options outside of black universities. HBCUs got a small boost in the 1980s, when Bill Cosby sensationalized black colleges with his hit sitcom, *A Different World*, which was at the fictitious black Hillman College. Sweatshirts emblazoned with black college logos became trendy. During those heady days, many HBCU graduates ended up pulling down big dollars on Wall Street, or engaging in important research at the National Institutes of Health, or as professors who had gone on to get their graduate degrees and were well prepared.

But since then, HBCUs have lost out to a wave of aggressive competitors, whether it is for-profits such as the University of Phoenix, community colleges, or mainstream public and private institutions. "So we are now left with a different quality of student," Taylor said.

To make his point, Taylor recounted an unpleasant—but in his view, entirely necessary—exchange he had recently with one of his scholarship students and his loving, supportive—if terribly misguided—mother. The young man had called Taylor's Washington, D.C., office panicked because he didn't have the proper attire for an upcoming job interview—a chance to work at a Fortune 500 company, which Taylor himself had arranged. That, in itself, wasn't a problem, as Taylor had plenty of vouchers for free suits, thanks to a subsidy deal with K&G, which boasted a line of suits designed by actor Blair Underwood. In essence, the Thurgood Marshall Fund had a deal with K&G in which they offered free business suits to young men in need.

Taylor was prepared to hand a voucher to the young man—that is, until he saw him stride into his office wearing a pair of spanking new $200 LeBron James sneakers. Taylor couldn't hide his outrage. "I said, 'Do you know what two hundred dollars would have gotten you at Joseph A. Bank? You could have gotten a sports coat, two pairs of pants, two shirts, and two ties. How do I look giving you something when I have truly needy people out here? You say you value this job and everything. You talk all of the rhetoric. But I can't help you.'" After the kid went home and complained to his mother, Taylor got an irate phone call. "You made my child come down to that damn office and you didn't give him this and . . ."

Taylor maintained his calm: "The number one question you have to ask is: How did you raise your child? Because his priorities are screwed up, priorities he's gotten from you. Instead of a two-hundred-dollar pair of shoes, you should have gotten him a suit. The problem is, you think everybody owes you and your child something. This is also a parenting problem. You sent your child over here to do this. You should have told him, 'Baby, don't wear them two-hundred-dollar sneakers up in there.' You, ma'am, have done him wrong."

This lack of accountability, or willingness to find fault in their own actions, extends to the HBCUs themselves. It's a hot-button issue for Taylor. From his vantage point, instead of spending so much time blaming others for our failing institutions, we should be doing the necessary work to fix them. White universities poach black talent because, in many cases, their offerings are simply more attractive, from scholarship packages to the quality of instruction. But HBCUs boast two million living alumni; if two million graduates pledged even a hundred dollars a year, HBCUs could build endowments all over the country. But for some reason, blacks refuse to fund our own schools.

"Where," Taylor asked rhetorically, "are the big black folks writing checks? Ask Bob Johnson, who has made a billion off of us. When has he made a major seven-figure-plus gift to anything black? Ask him. BET is a classic example of a business that made its money on people of color. And so imagine my level of surprise and disappointment when Sheila Johnson created a scholarship fund at Harvard; full tuition, plus a ten-thousand-dollar living stipend. Full tuition, living fees. Come on, you made your money in this community. I am trying to figure out why we're not giving. . . . Why is it that the white man's got to come write us a check all the time when we have enough wealth to support our own schools?"

Taylor went on: "Our funding comes from Republican rich white guys and their wives. It's generally not from among the large number of successful black folks who went to HBCUs. It's not who you would expect." Taylor chuckled at the irony, that the most generous donors were rarely African American—actually, in many cases, they were Jewish. One of his Jewish donors recently said to me, "Black people forget. We started the NAACP." This donor admitted that his largesse was more pragmatic than moral: Why should the government spend $30,000 a year incarcerating a black boy when educating him would lead to safer streets and improve his chances in the labor force?

But anyone, white or black, who writes a check to support an institution expects to see adequate performance. Taylor insists that in many cases, black colleges have handicapped themselves by not being discriminating in who they admit. In essence, the open enrollment policies practiced at many HBCUs are destroying the brand. "The best kids do not want to go to school with the worst kids."

As it stood, Taylor said, few HBCU leaders were willing to engage in a frank conversation about the quality of their students, at times even issuing outlandish comparisons to mainstream elite universities. As he recalled one president boasting recently: "You could put my top one percent up against that top one percent at Harvard." While Taylor listened politely, he couldn't help wondering whether the guy actually believed what he was saying.

Taylor understood that his views put him on a slippery slope with HBCU leaders; that his pronouncements on HBCU admission standards might come across as elitist. But his problem was not HBCUs accepting students who didn't necessarily fit the traditional profile of a college student. This has always been at the heart of the HBCU mission. Rather, Taylor took issue with HBCUs admitting students reading on an eighth-grade level, taking thousands of dollars from them during their four or five or six years at the college, and sending them out into the world not much better educated than when they arrived—in many cases, not even with a degree. "That's the new black on black crime," he said.

Clearly worked up now, Taylor offered an analogy to drive home his point. "Shooting somebody just means it's over. If I shoot you, you're dead. But if I take all your dreams, your money, your time, your mama's money through student loans, if I take all this stuff and you can't get a job, you'd have done better going to UPS and throwing boxes. You got debts, your mama got debts, and those things are not dischargeable in bankruptcy; that's black on black crime." Taylor shook his head pitifully.

"Or let's say you graduate them, and they go back to the community and they are unemployed or underemployed and all the other kids say, 'Hell, look what college got him.' And so now they don't aspire to go to college. You're doing more damage in the community. If you're going to take the unprepared or underprepared student, you have a moral obligation to make good on somebody investing twenty-five thousand dollars a year. That means over four years these kids have given you a hundred thousand dollars. If that kid has given you a hundred thousand dollars, his parents and grandparents and everybody else have made huge sacrifices. If that kid leaves your university unable to really compete in the job market, shame on you, shame on you. The white man ain't doing that to you. You can't blame him for that. The person who did that to you looked like you. They were the president of the university, the provost, the chancellor—that's who did it.

"I wish these university leaders would look at themselves and say,

'I shouldn't take this hundred thousand dollars from that kid because I can't get them ready. Maybe you should be in a vocational program, or a community college where you'll spend two years remediating and then come back here. But it's unfair for me to take your money.'"

The core of the problem, he said, was that HBCUs had lost their value position. "Some presidents will say we are the place where, if you can't get in any other school, you can get in here."

He laughed: "You'll never be considered a serious institution with that as your reputation. Then there are others who say we have a nurturing environment; we care and all that. That's interesting, but it's also incredibly soft. And then the third area is those who have said, we are going to be great universities, that's North Carolina A&T, that's FAMU."

North Carolina A&T boasts 10,000 students, more than any public HBCU in the nation, and one of the most lauded engineering programs in the country, black and white alike. Meanwhile, FAMU, or Florida Agricultural and Mechanical University, with 9,500 students, is also known for its top business and pharmacology programs. While these schools have explained their value proposition, many HBCUs have failed to offer a persuasive rationale for why they matter today. What within their narrative and curriculum makes them a better choice than a rival majority white university?

"When a student makes a decision to attend North Carolina A&T instead of the University of North Carolina, they shouldn't be compromising anything that comes with going to a major university, other than perhaps the brand recognition. Why would any kid in their right mind go to Fisk University when they've been accepted into the more selective Vanderbilt University?"

As Taylor saw it, the future of HBCUs, in reestablishing an identity, was consolidation—in pooling the limited resources of disparate black colleges into more competitive institutions. The idea was gaining traction in several state governments, but not without resistance from black legislators. No matter that mainstream institutions such as the University of Georgia had cut expenses by folding eight institutions into four. Black leaders in Georgia, for example, scoffed at proposals to merge the HBCU Albany State with nearby majority-white Darton State.

In North Carolina, for example, there was growing talk in the state senate about merging 123-year-old HBCU Elizabeth City State University with other state schools. Many Republican legislators viewed this as the best prescription for a school hemorrhaging students—from 3,300 in 2010 to 2,400 students in 2013—and faced a $5 million budget shortfall. A few years prior, Jackson State's president, Ronald Mason Jr., floated the idea of consolidating the state's HBCUs and critics nearly ran him out of town. Mason ultimately landed at Southern University in Louisiana, where the state's governor, Bobby Jindal, had been a longtime advocate of merging HBCUs.

Johnny Taylor said mergers and consolidations were fighting words to black college leaders because, in many cases, they preferred having their own fiefdoms rather than doing what was smart economically. "They're okay with having six presidents and six campuses and six technology infrastructure systems all within driving distance of each other," he said.

Near Xenia, Ohio, for example, private Wilberforce University was directly across the street from Central State University, one of the Thurgood Marshall College Fund schools. Central State enrolls about 2,100 students, while Wilberforce's enrollment is down to some 500 students, from 1,170 a decade ago. Most middle schools are even larger than that. There's been talk about Central State and Wilberforce merging for years, but only talk. The standoff strains credulity: Why would kids want to spend $20,000 at Wilberforce, when they can get a Central State education for $8,000?

Similarly, of North Carolina's eleven historically black colleges, six are private and all but one enroll fewer than two thousand students. That means if you combined all the state's private HBCUs into one entity, it would still be smaller than North Carolina A&T, in Greensboro, which boasts nearly eleven thousand students. Even more, those private HBCUs each charges tuition upward of $25,000. To mostly deaf ears, Taylor has proposed creating one university with five campuses specializing in various disciplines. Bennett College, the all-girls school in Greensboro, in nursing; Livingstone College in Salisbury would emphasize its engineering; and so on. How else to compete with the University of North Carolina, which has seventeen campuses throughout its state, five of which are HBCUs? It was a simple business strategy; even the region's grocers, Harris Teeter and Kroger, had merged.

In Florida, Bethune-Cookman University could brand itself as experts in teaching hospitality—the Johnson & Wales of the HBCU space—meanwhile the public university Florida Memorial could promote itself as a draw for studying international business, especially South American and Latin American, and even require Spanish as part of the curriculum.

Essentially, Taylor believes tiny, underfunded HBCUs like Bethune-Cookman urgently need to figure out ways to distinguish their academic offerings and value propositions to compete with the more robust state or regional rival of, say, the University of Miami, with its 16,000 students and 180 majors and programs.

There were some rumblings of mergers. For example, after losing its accreditation in 2011, St. Paul's College, located in Lawrenceville, Virginia, began merger talks with Saint Augustine's University, the small Raleigh, North Carolina–based liberal arts college founded in 1867. The plan would have dramatically expanded Saint Augustine's geographic and academic footprint but required, among other things, that Saint Augustine's assume St. Paul's some $5 million in debt. In the deal, St. Paul's nearly 150-acre campus would have remained unchanged, but the institution would be an extension of Saint Augustine's, along with its programs—which would have expanded to include business administration, criminal justice, teacher education, and rural community development—with degrees awarded by Saint Augustine's. But, in the end, talks between the Episcopal Church–affiliated schools became bogged down and eventually fell apart. As Saint Augustine's president Dianne Boardley Suber put it in a statement: "This is a very difficult decision to make. We explored several options after completing our due diligence. We concluded that the acquisition of Saint Paul's College at this time would significantly challenge the fiscal stability of Saint Augustine's University." That fall, the 125-year-old St. Paul's began shuttering its operations.

But Taylor was having trouble selling his consolidation argument to black college leaders. He worried that failing to change the business model would be a costly, if not fatal, mistake for these institutions. At Johnson C. Smith University, consultants from the Blue Ocean Strategy Network had spent months talking to the faculty, administrators, and students about their experiences at the university and had come away with a rather dire diagnosis. They said students had a bumpy and often unproductive experience from the moment they set foot on campus as freshmen. They said the university needed to do a better job during the orientation process, counseling them, tutoring them, engaging them for their future careers, and preparing them in the classroom for graduate school or the workplace. They said the school spent too much money on unnecessary programs—even the football team, and rather gingerly recommended we consider jettisoning it. This idea generated something close to laughter. The criticisms were difficult to hear, and perhaps even more so because the messengers were white. Their views, no matter how diplomatically delivered, were often taken as indictments of the university. The result was a defensive posture among many at the school as Blue Ocean displayed their PowerPoint presentations of colorful graphs, charts, and other metrics showing a lagging performance of basic functions and expectations. The consultants' overall sentiment was that most HBCUs were charging too much tuition for what was being offered, and the schools needed to measurably improve the product to compete more favorably in the overall higher education marketplace. We swallowed hard at this conclusion and nodded amicably. Behind closed doors we blamed our interlopers for their failure to understand and appreciate the value of HBCUs, that 3 percent of the nation's schools were, for instance, producing 50 percent of the engineers in black America.

But as Johnny Taylor put it: "Yeah, but the white colleges are saying, 'Sure you educated fifty percent, but the ten percent we educated are running things now'; they are saying: 'The best didn't come from you, they came from us. That's right, we graduate the Johnny Taylors of the world.'"

Oprah Winfrey attends Spelman College's 2012
commencement at Georgia International Convention
Center in Atlanta.

(*Rick Diamond/Getty Images*)

CHAPTER 7

DIVERSITY WEEKEND

NOW AND THEN, SAVANNAH BOWEN WOULD NO-
tice Miss Cadet-Simpkins around school, chatting with a student in
the hallway, whisking through the administrative offices, at events
in the gymnasium. She recalled, too, that her younger sister, Averie,
who had taken an English class under Miss Cadet-Simpkins, had
only positive things to say about her. Miss Cadet-Simpkins surely
stood out among the teachers at Pelham Memorial High School, not
only because she was black, but for faculty she had a unique sense of
style. Her dreadlocks, cool, patterned blouses, and funky jewelry
gave off a youngish, bohemian flair offset by a trusty frumpiness
that bespoke a good, freethinking English teacher.

It is always a stroke of good fortune when a teenager encounters
an adult who somehow manages to break through their armor and
inspire them to take a hard look at themselves and their place in the
world. Having mostly attended schools where she was surrounded
by white teachers and students, Savannah had purposely avoided
thinking much about how surviving such an atmosphere might have
affected her own identity, what weight she carried in order to succeed. She was wise enough to know that such introspection, too
much pondering about race and all its unfairness, could spawn self-
doubt or even bitterness. But when Savannah enrolled in Advanced
Placement English in the fall of 2011, the start of her senior year, she
felt an instant connection to her teacher, Miss Cadet-Simpkins, an

intellectual who, like Savannah's mother, was Haitian. And she sensed that it was life changing.

A star student throughout her school years, Savannah's routine was to sit up front in class, always on the teacher's right-hand side. The habit had started back in grade school when her teachers tended to seat pupils in alphabetical order, and since Savannah had rarely strayed from such close proximity to her teachers, it served the dual purpose of helping her to focus while emphasizing her presence. While Savannah was psyched about the course, most of her other two-dozen classmates had enrolled for no other than the practical reason of beefing up their high school transcript with another advanced placement course.

In the classroom, Miss Cadet-Simpkins was an easygoing but no-nonsense taskmaster who worked her students hard with lots of quizzes, in-class writing assignments, and reading homework. They studied and recited poetry, particularly Shakespeare, learning to understand the nuances of meter, particularly iambic pentameter. They read lots of classic novels; from Emily Brontë's *Wuthering Heights*, to Charles Dickens's *Great Expectations*, to *As I Lay Dying* by William Faulkner.

Miss Cadet-Simpkins was not one to play favorites, and if she felt a similar pull toward Savannah, she let it unfold naturally. Their bonding moment came early on when she asked her students, virtually all of whom were college bound, to submit their college application essays for one-on-one review during her office hours. Savannah had written two essays: one on her conflicted feelings about playing tennis, and another about a recent trip to Haiti in which she volunteered to help schools recover following the devastating 2010 earthquake. She decided to share her Haiti essay, which told of the country's hardship and courage; how her mom and dad worked with hospitals to offer physical examinations to hundreds who needed medical assistance, how she led a fund-raising campaign for her French club to purchase benches for schools because students, many who literally crossed rivers to get to school, had nowhere to sit once they arrived. Miss Cadet-Simpkins praised the work as authentic, and not another generic, third-world travelogue.

In talking with Miss Cadet-Simpkins about her essay (she ended up selecting the tennis essay about living life on her own terms, which she felt was stronger), Savannah also shared her college plans; most of her friends were headed to the Ivy League, or to elite private liberal arts colleges. Savannah was strongly considering Macalester College, a small, highly ranked liberal arts school in Saint Paul, Minnesota. Macalester was courting her aggressively; the college had offered to fly her to Saint Paul to tour the campus during its "diversity weekend" and meet the tennis team. Miss Cadet-Simpkins could relate to being a sought-after academic achiever; she herself had chosen Yale University for undergraduate school, but after two years had transferred to Spelman College.

Savannah didn't talk to her about her painfully awkward social life, but she wanted to. As a varsity tennis player, she occupied a privileged space at the school, but it always felt complicated by race. The sad truth was that most of her white classmates at Pelham seemed to view black students as second-class, misdirected, negative influences. She felt pressure from her white friends to avoid them. "It was like, if you want to preserve your social status you can't befriend them," she said. "It was pressure. To be the best black girl you can be, and not be like other black kids. I was young and not really able to make sense of that, how to internalize it without thinking that I'm somehow different."

No longer the shy, gangly adolescent, Savannah had sprouted into a tall, attractive young woman. She had attended an all-girls school for middle school and was unaccustomed to the romantic advances of boys. While she still wasn't interested in dating—her dad wouldn't approve anyway—she had become curious and didn't mind the flirtations of potential suitors as long as they were polite. There was, for instance, one black guy who always made a point of speaking to her, and who seemed to be sizing her up to ask her out on a date, but her white friends quickly dismissed him as a bad guy with girlfriends all over town. Savannah caved and stayed away from him.

Her visit during that fall to Macalester, her dream school, seemed to promise a similar social conundrum. Tucked away within the bustling heart of Saint Paul, Minnesota, its old redbrick buildings and canopies of leafy maples wrapped the campus in Old World quaintness, and evoked virtually everything Savannah wanted in a college. It was small, with two thousand students, with a robust curriculum and top-notch faculty whose accolades had earned the university international acclaim. Although most of her friends were applying to such eastern Ivy League schools as Harvard, Princeton, and Brown, they knew about Macalester, which held its own special kind of cachet as small, elite, and highly competitive. She was blown away to learn that among Macalester's graduates was Nobel Peace Prize recipient Kofi Annan, the Ghanaian diplomat and former United Nations secretary-general.

Yet what struck Savannah was that up close Macalester hardly reflected the diversity boasted in its glossy brochures. The university's reputation as a bastion of white privilege was a kind of open secret. For the past few years, for instance, Macalester had been engaged in a nasty legal battle with one of its own faculty members, a Chinese immigrant English professor who had filed a discrimination lawsuit against the university after being denied a promotion. Wang Ping, an award-winning author of ten published books, alleged in a 2012 lawsuit filed with the U.S. Equal Employment Opportunity Commission that despite her strong credentials and a stellar record of teaching and service at Macalester, she was turned down for a promotion, while a white colleague with fewer credentials at the university applied for and received an early promotion. She also claimed that after appealing the decision, Macalester officials began retaliating by slashing funding for her teaching, student publications, and classroom work, even withdrawing support for her most important scholarly work, the Kinship of Rivers project.

"Why is Macalester so punitive, so unwilling to consider a better work relation? I can't answer," Ping posted in a blog lamenting the turn of events at Macalester. "All I know is that I kicked the hornet's nest by complaining about the administrators' unequal treatments and retaliation. I always know that as a woman and a Chinese immigrant, I have to work harder and achieve more in every aspect: scholarship, teaching, and service, in order to survive academia, especially at Macalester with its record of high minority faculty turnover. . . ."

During her trip to Macalester, Savannah walked around campus all day and encountered what seemed like only a handful of non-white students. She was quite deflated when she attended a black literature course to find an old white man lecturing to the class. When the class was dismissed, she approached a young black woman, the only other black student in the room, and inquired about what seemed a cultural mismatch. The response, the girl's defeated shrug of her shoulders, spoke volumes.

But if Macalester's lily-white culture gave her pause, the university's hefty tuition of nearly $50,000 per year worried her most. A Division III school, Macalester wasn't offering her a tennis scholarship, and the financial aid figure they came up with would mean tens of thousands out of pocket or in loans during her four years there. Even more, Savannah's two younger sisters would soon need college support, too, and it would have been unfair for Savannah to overburden their parents financially when there were plenty of other great, less-expensive colleges she could attend. As the plane departed the Twin Cities, Savannah had already begun rethinking her plans.

Morehouse College's 2013 graduates listen to
President Barack Obama deliver his commencement
address in the rain.

(*Mandel Ngan/AFP/Getty Images*)

CHAPTER 8

OBAMA AND THE MOREHOUSE MEN

WHEN PRESIDENT OBAMA MADE HIS WAY ONTO the stage at Morehouse College that rainy morning in May, his appearance was, without a doubt, a sight for the ages, a moment brimming with all sorts of historical significance. But his tough-love message was lost on many, including a number of black scribes. In them, the message triggered a fair amount of outrage. As *Washington Post* columnist Courtland Milloy opined, " . . . the president all but discounted their achievements, injecting the unseemly specter of a 'poverty of ambition' and raising the insulting prospect of their interests becoming limited to shopping sprees."

To many leaders in the HBCU community, the speech reaffirmed their suspicion that the president was not only dangerously condescending and disconnected from the plight of African Americans, but also not willing to hold government accountable for long-standing policies that have contributed to racial performance gaps. Among those incensed by what he viewed as the president's lack of effective leadership toward black students was Johnny Taylor, head of the Thurgood Marshall College Fund. "Martin Luther King Jr., Malcolm X—all of them have to be turning over in their graves to see that all of this is happening under an African American president," he told me. Taylor lamented that Obama, despite winning a second term (largely on the votes of African Americans), had proved virtually impotent in tackling America's black male crisis; the high rates of incarceration, drug abuse, unemployment, violent crime. Even whites agreed that the black male crisis was a national problem, and would likely support a prescriptive legislation, he said. "Yet where's the big program, the big initiative?" Taylor asked.

Obama's acquiescence extended to HBCUs, he said. Taylor had grown weary of the lopsided logic spewed by critics of black colleges, and he blamed Obama for not stepping up to correct it. He was tired of hearing about how Americans had invested billions in HBCUs and how the return had been weakening in recent years. How, they asked, could taxpayers justify burning more money on them? Taylor usually responded with another question: How could the president invest in saving General Motors, Bank of America, AIG—all of those organizations burned through significantly more money than HBCUs would ever get an opportunity to spend. And they had the best Harvard-trained staff and CEOs. They had corporate jets and corporate cars, you name it, and they screwed up royally. Yet the president bailed them out because he decided that they were too important to fail. Why is it that HBCUs, a group of American institutions that have been historically underfunded, do not merit the same consideration? Why hadn't Obama drawn a line in the sand and proclaimed that HBCUs were too important to fail?

It seemed outrageous to Taylor that the Obama administration had assumed the neutral posture of allowing these historic institutions to simply fade into extinction. When GM was failing a few years prior, Obama handed them a big check with the caveat of a forced corporate restructuring. He essentially fired GM's president and half the company's board. Why not do the same for HBCUs? Why not intervene and say, I want these universities to survive: here's a hundred million dollars, but the way you do business has got to change. HBCUs employ thousands of people, pay millions in taxes, graduate 50 percent of the black engineers, 75 percent of the black veterinarians, 50 percent of the black classroom teachers. In a society that is increasingly brown, the role of HBCUs is more important than ever. Yet President Obama seemed to have turned his back on HBCUs.

On commencement day, Morehouse president John Silvanus Wilson felt some vindication against Obama's critics. He understood some of the backlash, as he had spent three years as director of the White House Initiative on Historically Black Colleges and Universities, and was well aware of the bungled rollout of the revisions to the Direct PLUS Loan program. And he could offer no real defense of the situation, or the angst it was causing in black higher education, except to say that the policy change was not about targeting HBCUs. The crisis was simply the result of a rule shift made in general terms that unfortunately had a disproportionate impact— one that the Department of Education should have foreseen. It was also true that Wilson, despite his key role, was little more than a bit player in this drama. Just as the controversy was brewing, Wilson had begun private talks with the Morehouse search committee for the university president job and therefore had to recuse himself from all discussions.

As for Johnny Taylor's criticism, as it happened, Wilson and Taylor claimed each other as friends. Wilson regarded Taylor as smart, and far more in touch with the facts than most others he had dealings with while working for Obama. Taylor proved both an informed critic of the administration at times, and also an informed supporter, but he was always informed. Wilson did disagree with Taylor's rather critical characterization of the president's policy on HBCUs.

The facts spoke for themselves: Shortly after Barack Obama became president, the amount of money coming from the federal government into HBCUs was a little less than $4 billion every year. By the time Wilson left the White House at the end of the president's first term, some $5.3 billion had gone into HBCUs under the president. Before Barack Obama came into office, Pell grant support of HBCUs came in at less than a half billion annually; by the end of the first Obama term, Pell grant support to HBCUs more than doubled to a billion dollars a year.

Finally, just before Barack Obama took office, President Bush in his last two years had pushed about $85 million a year into HBCUs, a supplement that was expiring as Obama took office. Obama, instead of renewing the funds for a couple more years, committed to another ten years of funding at the same level, or $850 million over a decade. The data simply failed to support any notion of Barack Obama engaged in a war against HBCUs. Those HBCU leaders who complained about what the federal government had done or failed to do for black colleges, particularly under President Obama, were not in touch with the facts. More often, their gripes were rooted in the fragile egos bruised in Obama's push to hold HBCUs, along with all publicly funded colleges and universities, more accountable for their performances.

Beverly Daniel Tatum, president of Spelman College, who served on the White House Initiative and was equally defensive of the president, said it best: "The questions that are being asked about graduation rates are not being targeted specifically at HBCUs. When the president talks about accountability, he's not just talking about HBCUs. Every college has to ask, 'Why aren't our students graduating? What is interfering from beginning to end with them getting that degree?' I don't blame President Obama for asking a question about graduation rates in a country where one out of two students graduate. It is not an unreasonable question when he asks how colleges are meeting the nation's needs for college graduates. But there is this sensitivity because institutions that have particularly low graduation rates, they know it's a vulnerability."

She continued: "But if you have students who come in and need remediation, it's going to take them a long time to graduate. Students who can't afford to pay and can't get financial aid may have to step out and work. There is data that shows that if you are a low-income first-generation college student you are more likely to experience a family death during the course of your college education than your white middle-class counterpart. So there are all kinds of hurdles that you have to overcome that are working against you. The fact is that many HBCUs offer an environment where people are rooting for you and saying, 'You are going to graduate,' because they know who these kids are and where they are coming from. And all these things HBCUs have done because they know where these kids are coming from . . ."

If John Silvanus Wilson was short on fans, among his biggest was Dr. John Williams, his old Morehouse professor, a forceful but amiable sort who had recently retired as chair of the university's business school. A Morehouse alum himself, class of 1974, Williams joined the Morehouse faculty in the 1970s and was credited with transforming a sleepy business and finance program into a kind of academic juggernaut, a prestigious gateway for black males to become big ballers on Wall Street. If Florida A&M was known for graduating legions of talented aspiring corporate managers, Morehouse became a training ground for private equity dealmakers. His success was unparalleled: in most years, the university boasted an 80 percent placement rate for graduates.

Under Williams's tough tutelage, which blended rigorous analytical training with strong argumentative and presentational skills, most business department grads were either snapped up by such premier Wall Street firms as Goldman Sachs or Lehman Brothers, or went on to garner MBAs at Harvard or Wharton. Along the way, Dr. Williams—or "J Dub" as his students fondly called him—earned a reputation as a high-impact teacher and administrator—something of a rare breed these days in HBCUs, since the most talented academicians tend to get plucked away onto mainstream campuses. As among the first to groom large numbers of young black men to succeed on Wall Street—to think and talk like an investment banker, and to dress like one—Williams has become a kind of folk hero in the industry. "We've been placing brothers on the Street since the mid-seventies," Williams announced one sunny Saturday afternoon. Wearing jeans, a polo shirt, and a burgundy Morehouse cap, he was dressed to cheer on Morehouse against the Howard Bisons at the Nation's Football Classic at RFK Stadium later that afternoon. He was also looking forward to spending a bit of social time with Wilson in the president's skybox. He offered a counterpoint to questions about the market value of an HBCU degree.

"So we already told our students that they can do it, that they have a history, that all your big brothers have been doing this for years. Back then, there were very few blacks working on the Street. Morehouse was among the first undergraduate schools, not just HBCUs, to place kids in investment banking right out of undergraduate school. Of course, there were those from majority schools in the East, whose uncles or fathers were high executives in banking and could say, 'You hire my niece, I'll hire your nephew.' But we didn't have those kinds of networks. We had to go there and present ourselves and hope to get called back. Chase was the first one that started recruiting us, and then it just spread to all the banks and so forth when word got around that 'these are good kids.' "

The result, Williams continued, was that black parents began to broaden their thinking about lucrative careers for their children to pursue, and to view Morehouse as a springboard to a financial fast track. "We once steered our students to be physicians and lawyers because of the prestige. As blacks, we were trying to get both prestige and money through one generation. It's still wonderful to become a physician, but where our community used to associate that with higher earning, that's no longer the case. It's wonderful to become a corporate senior manager, too. I have some kids who will go work on the Street and in those firms make in their bonus what the guy at Owens Corning makes overall in a whole year. That's not including their signing bonus. A lot of money is made up there on the Street. You're talking about the top two or three percent of earners in the world. I think our community has begun to understand that you don't get much higher than that. But I've always taught my students that after finance, you can only go to heaven."

Williams added: "Of course, that's one thing Morehouse grads love to do—come back to campus in nice suits and tell students about all the deals they just did in London and Johannesburg," he said, chuckling. "But they also tell them, you've still gotta know what beta is and how to derive beta. You can't just talk a good game. And just knowing beta still is not gonna get it. You've gotta know how to present to your supervisors and peers. So our students understand that you've gotta know your stuff."

Mostly, though, students credit Williams with preparing them to battle those invisible demons that tend to lurk in the crevices of a high-risk, high-reward industry such as investment banking, a culture known as much for its grinding work schedules as its good-old-boy, often cutthroat exclusivity. "That's our challenge—making sure our students can survive in these big multinational firms," he said. "Many HBCUs don't have that problem; they might be placing one or two students here or there per year, but they're not going to get thirty and forty a year for interning, or fifteen, thirty, or forty permanent jobs with the multinationals. So we have to teach them, it's more than just being smart. You need to be confident. You got to have the emotional framework. You've got to put the hours in, not only to get the GPA to get noticed, but also when you get to work. In those kinds of institutions, you don't look to see when it's five o'clock. Knock-off time is for rank and file, not the professional class. The professional class doesn't knock off; they finish the project. There are a number of HBCUs that have the students who are capable of achieving comparable achievements, but they may not have the exposure and confidence to survive on the Street. They have the mental ability but maybe not the emotional framework yet."

For instruction, Williams relies heavily on the Socratic method, favoring a volley of facts and ideas between students and faculty over more rigid, less interactive approaches to teaching. Williams, typically calm in talking pedagogy, gets passionate about this topic. "It's not just about the classical lecture—'you take my notes and my exam'—no, no, no! It's more than that," he said. "We're developing presentation skills; we require a lot of group work and group evaluations. Students complain because if they've got a lot of slackers in the group, the whole grade goes down. Well, that's the real world, that's the labor market. That's business.

"We have open discussions. I use the Socratic method because it requires you to think on your feet. You can't come and sit there and think everything is going to be okay because you read the text. In fact, not only are you called on at random, but even if you prepared yourself and your answer is correct, you're then cross-examined on that answer—well, what about 'this,' or what if 'that' was the case? You're developing this confidence as you go. You also cultivate the students to cross-examine each other, to say 'I disagree with his answer' because he left out this or that. So it's no longer you against Mr. Teacher or Ms. Teacher; you're competing against each other in the classroom. It's like a friendly kind of boot camp."

Unfortunately, he said, most HBCUs curriculums today do not emphasize discussion and debate. "For most schools, and I say certainly of the HBCU deans I know, the classical model is students go in and listen to a lecture, they take an exam. If you want to get a B or an A, you better get an average that comes up to that. They're not worried about group evaluations or presentation skills, and all those kinds of things. There's not a lot of discussion in class. This whole notion of you can train successful business students by just lecturing and taking notes, that's not going to get you there."

Williams encouraged faculty to focus less on grades and more on academic rigor, not only through the complexity of the workload but the sheer volume of it. "We try not to play the gatekeeper," he said. "We try to approach it like an Ivy League school. You think these Ivy League schools attract all these good students to give them

Cs and Ds and Fs? No, no, no—that's not how they approach it. They'll work the hell out of you, which is how they are able to stay until ten, eleven o'clock at night. It's because they are used to it. They're used to the volume. With enough volume, I can ensure learning, and then I can assign an A or a B and still say 'I haven't given you a thing because I made you work for it.'"

The Morehouse student today views hard work—and expectations of it from professors—quite differently than when he joined the faculty, Williams said. "Back then, the labor market was just opening up to African Americans, we're talking about multinational jobs, even big accounting," he said. "Their expectations were not as high or as clear, and they assumed that there was a direct correlation between work ethic and success. If you worked hard, these companies would hire you and you'd do well. Now, the notion is 'I come, I'm here, and if I keep my nose clean, I'll do well.' There's an entitlement mentality. It's 'I expect to get a big job.' I don't know if they recognize the correlation between hard work and grades and getting a good job. I think they think, 'I'm here and if I can get through this I'll succeed.' But faculty members can handle that early on. The answer is in volume: plenty of reading, plenty of writing, lots of problems."

Williams, who took charge of Morehouse's business department in 1982 and retired in 2013, has worked to create a culture that challenges faculty to do more than tabulate passing and failing grades in their courses. "I challenge my professors: 'Why are students doing poorly in your corporate finance class? If I taught them, they'd have more As and Bs. What is it that you're *not* doing correctly? You need another approach. This isn't a time to flunk folks; this is a time to get people to learn, motivate them to learn, find a way to make sure they learn.'"

He also pushes students to get a passport and travel—in many cases with Morehouse faculty. For nearly three decades, Williams has taken a few faculty members and a couple dozen students on weeklong international tours during which they visited and studied the markets in two or three countries. "Let them see the world," he said. "Even in our earliest days, we exposed our students by putting them on a plane to New York as freshmen and sophomores and taking them to the New York Stock Exchange, and to meet all the big companies. They got to shake hands and put on their ties. And the companies started to like them and bring them up for internships and hiring. But more importantly, the kids got exposure and it built their confidence."

Williams liked to tell the story of a business school dean at a major university who reached out to him a few years ago looking for advice on bolstering its national profile and student placement rate. They were impressed by Morehouse business school's graduates and wanted the recipe for the secret sauce. "Now, these are white administrators coming to me, trying to figure out how they can start," Williams said. "I gave them some pointers and they started a program that takes them up to Wall Street. Just to give you an idea of what it takes, they sent me a picture published in the local newspaper of the group that went to Wall Street, and I noticed one in the group was a black guy. It was their first time, but this is how little they knew about the Street, how little training they had: the black guy was standing there wearing a red shirt. The only black guy. None of them were really dressed in the corporate attire we would have worn, the dark suits and black shoes. Our students would have known how to dress. But the black male in the group had on a red shirt. He was probably from a modest background. And the administrators didn't feel comfortable telling him when he showed up or they assumed that he would have known better and didn't tell him. Anyway, it was too late. But I looked at that picture and said to myself, what does this really have to do with race? Nothing. This has everything to do with exposure."

Xavier University of Louisiana student Tritan Brown
studies in the university's common area.

(Gerald Herbert/AP)

CHAPTER 9

THE HIP-HOP PRESIDENT

SMARTPHONE IN HAND, DR. WALTER KIMBROUGH,
the decidedly hip president of Dillard University, was sitting in an
auditorium at the University of Michigan scrolling through his
Twitter feed when he came across the news: rap impresario Dr. Dre
had just awarded $35 million, half of a $70 million gift given with
his business partner Danny Iovine, to the University of Southern
California. Kimbrough was floored. In a few moments, he was to
speak to a student affairs group at U of M about creating a diverse
campus culture, and so Kimbrough put aside thoughts about this
fairly phenomenal gift to focus on the lecture ahead of him.

But later that mid-May afternoon, as Kimbrough strode through
Detroit Metropolitan Airport, headed back to his campus in New
Orleans, he felt his frustration rising. He was startled by his own reaction, how quickly his initial pride that Dr. Dre had just awarded the
largest gift by an African American to higher education turned to
outrage. Perhaps he shouldn't have been: after all, Kimbrough's love
for rap music has earned him the moniker "the Hip-Hop President."

Walking through the airport, Kimbrough began counting black
people wearing Beats headphones, the company co-owned by Dr.
Dre. He thought to himself, Wow, here's this black man who was a
catalyst in hip-hop, a key figure in selling the African American
image and allowing whites to live vicariously through black people,
through hip-hop, yet he gives this big gift to this white school. Not

just any white school, but USC (or as he dubbed it, the University of Spoiled Children), which boasted a $4 or $5 billion endowment, assets that were in large part donated to the university. Kimbrough sat down and read more about the gift, and tried to console himself with the thought that Dre's largesse was something less than philanthropic, but rather a kind of seed capital to fund an incubator to develop students who would come work for Beats after graduating. He saw Dre's gift as purely opportunistic, which was in itself disappointing.

The longer Kimbrough pondered the gift, the more irritated he became. Awaiting his flight at the airport, he began tapping out a letter that would be published as an op-ed in the *Los Angeles Times*. He wrote: "What if Dre had given $35 million—his half of the USC gift and about 10 percent of his wealth, according to a Forbes estimate—to an institution that enrolls the very people who supported his career from the beginning? An institution where the majority of students are low-income? A place where $35 million would represent a truly transformational gift?" In the letter, Kimbrough noted other donors to black colleges; the $20 million gift (still the largest private donation given to an HBCU) Bill and Camille Cosby gave to Spelman College back in 1988; the $12 million Oprah Winfrey has gifted to Morehouse College; the $500,000 Sean "P. Diddy" Combs gave to his alma mater Howard University in 1999. "I can't help but wish that Dre's wealth, generated as it was by his largely black hip-hop fans, was coming back to support that community," Kimbrough wrote. Kimbrough told me that he tried to reach out later to Dre for a meeting, but to no avail.

What most bothered Kimbrough was that Dre, like most any other informed black person, was surely well aware that black colleges' largest obstacle is financial resources, that the number of kids at USC who qualify for Pell grants is 24 percent, while Dillard's students hover near 75 percent. Even more, corporations weren't giving as much money to HBCUs these days, and foundations and individuals, too, were much stingier with their dollars.

The tightened purse strings left Kimbrough with little choice but to try to grow his own base of student donors by making sure Dillard's graduates left so pleased by their experience that, in say, thirty or forty years, they'd be writing big checks to the university.

Much of the challenge simply came down to family wealth—or rather blacks' lack of it. According to industry estimates, it would cost more than $1 billion to gift every HBCU with a $10 million endowment. To put that into perspective, the nation's twenty wealthiest African Americans hold a combined net worth of about $9 billion, compared to the five richest European Americans, who boast approximately $235 billion.

Dillard had always been viewed as among the so-called Black Ivys, along with Fisk, Hampton, Howard, Spelman, and Morehouse. Dillard still enjoyed a formidable reputation among HBCUs, but was still recovering from the devastation of Hurricane Katrina, which required millions in rebuilding funds. The crisis had forced Dillard into some necessary soul-searching about the best way to compete against the new realities in higher education; to ask, what's our niche?; what's our value proposition?

During meetings with other HBCU leaders, Kimbrough often felt like the odd man out. His colleagues seemed stuck in the past, complaining about government cuts and lamenting about how things were done three or four decades ago. He, though, was eager to search for new ideas to reinvent tired old models. He had only been a university president for nine years, so he knew no other way—his experience had been tumultuous from the start.

Kimbrough was thirty-seven when he was tapped as president of Philander Smith College in Little Rock, Arkansas. The average age of a university president was fifty-eight, and the difference left him sitting at the proverbial kids' table. At one of his first United Negro College Fund meetings, he remembered taking issue with some numerical projections one of the presidents had presented and speaking up about it, yet being ignored. Then one of the presidents interjected: We got these young people coming in and they think they can talk; we're like a fraternity, and they think they can talk in the room with the giants. Kimbrough knew exactly who the giants were; they were the late Benjamin Mays at Morehouse; Johnnetta B. Cole, the former president of Spelman; and William Harvey, president of Hampton University. This guy, who had been booted from two universities, once amid allegations of sexual harassment, was hardly a giant. Kimbrough was pissed.

He went to his room to get dressed for a formal banquet later that evening, but not before calling his wife and telling her half-jokingly to get the bail money together, because he might go to jail after beating up the loudmouth. But when he put on his tuxedo and went to the reception looking to confront him, one of the veteran HBCU presidents who witnessed the awkward exchange approached him and told him not to be offended by what happened. At fifty, he had already been through his hazing. God sent me the right person that day, Kimbrough liked to say, and helped him adjust to the culture of the office—all the way down to its fraternal pettiness.

Since then, Kimbrough had found his way among the dinosaurs: he viewed himself as a disciple of Benjamin Mays, but was less interested in having buildings named after him than in understanding students' goals and building programs that empowered them to reach those goals. His day-to-day mission was clear: build new centers of excellence at Dillard that expanded the university's strengths. While Dillard, for instance, ranked at the top among HBCUs in physics and nursing, and in science, technology, engineering, and math (or STEM subjects) generally, he needed to create signature programs that enhanced Dillard's brand, like premed and pharmacy were to neighboring HBCU Xavier University, or heck, like football was to LSU.

One opportunity was Dillard's film program, what with New Orleans at the center of a burgeoning "Hollywood South." He knew that Howard was pulling out of its film program, and saw an opportunity to fill that gap. It didn't hurt either that the state of Louisiana was offering generous tax credits to film producers. Spike Lee had tapped several Dillard students to intern on his movie set, and he even came to speak on a couple of occasions.

He knew this work was urgent, despite those critics arguing that HBCUs were unnecessary in these racially integrated times. Sure, students could attend anywhere. But there was a price to pay in going to an institution that, upon its creation, prohibited you from attending and failed to recognize your humanity.

Kimbrough had been thinking quite a bit lately about those critics, and about what he viewed as a kind of fake outrage about why black colleges even exist today, from those who propose getting rid of them. But he had recently read a Harvard University study on the fiftieth anniversary of *Brown v. Board of Education*, which basically said the nation's K–12 is resegregating and getting back to pre–*Brown v. Board* levels. He thought, So it's okay for people to live in segregated neighborhoods, go to segregated primary and secondary schools, and then all of a sudden you want to get rid of HBCUs. "But then after college we go back to our segregated churches in our segregated neighborhoods. So if you want to get rid of HBCUs, we ought to push to get rid of segregated K–12 because then students would say 'I don't want to go to a black institution.' Deal with it on that level. So when people are old enough to make choices, then you want to take that away. Nobody is beating a drum for integrated elementary schools."

Kimbrough wanted HBCU leaders to push back harder against critics, to hold mainstream colleges more accountable for making universities more welcoming and engaging for black students and improving their graduation rates. He wouldn't mind putting HBCUs out of business if that was the approach.

Meanwhile, though, HBCU leaders needed to step up their game. He believed many of his colleagues had fallen these days to pushing academic gimmicks, and in time would pay dearly for it. Among the biggest gimmicks being hustled was the big push in online education.

Kimbrough was a skeptic about investing heavily in online education—which was ironic considering that he embraced technology more than most presidents, relying on Twitter, Facebook, Instagram, and other social media to get Dillard's message out. Unlike many of his colleagues, though, he didn't view technology as panacea for learning, especially for HBCU students. Perhaps it was a helpful tool, but not much more than that.

He didn't buy the hype either that online education would help boost enrollment or academic performance.

What's more, the push was occurring without any research on

the first-generation, low-income people of color HBCUs served. His students needed teachers working closely with them, eyeballing assignments. What the research did show was that his students were not developing strong communication and people skills. They hid behind texting from their smart phones, and were much weaker in engaging with people face-to-face in real life.

Even more, the research suggested that unless the university fully adopted an online model, it was a waste of time and resources. How were you going to compete with a for-profit company like the University of Phoenix, when some 20 percent of its income was used for advertising on star spokesmen like Arizona Cardinal wide receiver Larry Fitzgerald, and the university spent more on advertising than it did on academics? You couldn't be halfway in online education and expect the same results. You couldn't dabble in it, as so many HBCUs were doing.

He was all for radical thinking and change. For instance, he applauded his colleague Beverly Daniel Tatum's move to cut intercollegiate sports at Spelman. The university saved itself some money on something students weren't excited about anyway. Plus, the advantage was that their students hadn't really lost anything; Spelman is so closely aligned with Morehouse that students were going to Morehouse games to enjoy sporting events anyway. What did they lose? Nothing. Tatum's move was brilliant.

But tiny black schools hoping to compete in online education seemed to him a pipe dream at best, and a tremendous waste of money at worst. Kimbrough was looking to create a kind of Starbucks experience, in which people were willing to spend big bucks to get a high-quality product unmatched in the market. He was willing to put in the hours to make it happen—instead of wasting his energy blaming the Obama administration. Unlike many of his fellow black college presidents, Kimbrough believed Obama was unfairly criticized for the weakening state of HBCUs. He remained a huge supporter of the president. In fact, Kimbrough's son's middle name was Barack, as he was born the day Obama was elected.

Instead, Kimbrough blamed the folks around Obama who lacked the proper sensibility for HBCUs to ensure they were on his radar. The Direct PLUS Loan program was a debacle that grew out of his insulation. Obama's intentions were strong from the start, as indicated by the ten-year, nearly billion-dollar budget for HBCUs. It was money Congress couldn't touch, mandatory spending. The recent lapses were not the president's doing at all, but rather that of the folks around him. And this was unfortunate. Just the other day, Kimbrough was in a meeting and the conversation was, We'd hate for the first black president's legacy to be the destruction of HBCUs. Because people are going to say that. If bad things happen, he is going to take the blame for it—especially if he didn't get the right people in his ear. Instead of Obama, HBCU presidents needed to take a hard look at their own operations—especially at their board of trustees.

Some five hundred miles south of Morehouse, Dottie Belletto, a middle-aged white woman and among New Orleans's top event planners, sat squarely at the messy intersection of race and higher education. For the past two years, she had been the promoter of the Bayou Classic, the languishing black college football rivalry game between Grambling State University and Southern University. She won the contract from the black firm Bickerstaff Sports & Entertainment, based in Washington, D.C., and there were still sour feelings among the black old guard that a white woman—no matter that she was local and well regarded—had taken over as the business face behind the Bayou Classic.

But even under her leadership, the Bayou Classic had proven tough to resuscitate, its popularity having slipped for the first time behind the Magic City Classic in Birmingham, Alabama, which, incidentally, was also being managed by a white firm. Belletto worried that, despite her expertise and deep connections throughout the city, the once-thriving Bayou Classic may have fallen too far in recent years for even her experienced team to rescue it. And in the process of trying, she was witnessing firsthand the hardships of marketing a black cause to white customers. "As a Caucasian business woman and a minority, in my own right, I could cry," she said one afternoon, sitting in her office. "It's very enlightening. No Caucasian could understand what a dark-skinned person has to deal with. I feel sometimes that we've gone back fifty years. The race issue is so prevalent everywhere. It's still there. It's hard to believe. I mean, fifty years ago, you were thinking that way. But today, really?"

Among her biggest obstacles was that HBCUs were either invisible, or plain irrelevant, to her white friends and contacts. Black colleges simply had never intersected with white lives in any meaningful way, even though these universities had been around for more than a century; Southern University and Grambling State University were founded in 1880 and 1901, respectively. White oblivion to such old, important institutions was, in her eyes, a kind of travesty, and required her, in many cases, to market the Bayou Classic under the assumption that the event wasn't on the radar of even the city's biggest individual and corporate players. In her mind and at staff meetings, she found herself fretting: Have we done everything that we possibly could do; contacted everybody in our Rolodex, educated the public overall, especially whites, about what the Bayou Classic is all about, what the event really represents to Louisiana, to the nation?

Along with planning a pre-Classic parade to help promote the event locally, she constantly talked up the Classic to her wide circle of friends and associates, explaining that the big weekend was about more than pageantry, music, and parties; it was mostly about educating students. She relished those moments when she witnessed proof that her message was breaking through, like last year when, at the annual Battle of the Bands, she looked up into the crowd and recognized faces from the city's white uptown community. "Our senator Mary Landrieu was right there sitting in a front-row seat!"

Without a higher profile and broader community support, the Bayou Classic would continue fading. Instead of promoting it as a purely social event, Belletto had begun to create ancillary white-collar functions aimed at professional networking and workforce development. By her observation, black colleges had done a poor job of creating a strong pipeline for graduates to move into mid- and ultimately upper-level management positions. Offering venues where employers could meet and recruit black talent would not only bolster revenue, but make the Classic more relevant to whites and blacks alike. At its core, the Bayou Classic was less about entertainment—even though her staff had been in a frenzy negotiating to secure comedian Kevin Hart for the halftime show—

and more about economic development for students, schools, companies, and the city, and needed to be marketed as such.

To that end, she had worked hard to bring the city's business brass to the table, from the New Orleans Regional Black Chamber of Commerce to Greater New Orleans Inc. She was particularly surprised to discover many doors, in many cases belonging to deep-pocketed individuals, on which her marketing predecessors had never knocked. In the forty-one years of the Classic's existence, she was the first person to knock on the local NBC affiliate's door—although the affiliate had been broadcasting the game for sixteen years. Some would say this was low-hanging fruit, but she wanted to seal the deal and make it a partnership in hopes of getting the word out into the community.

Prior to Belletto taking over, neither the Downtown Development District nor the Chamber of Commerce had ever fully engaged in the Bayou Classic, nor had the Hotel and Lodging Association, the Louisiana Restaurant Association, or even the New Orleans Police Department. The goal was simply to coax more hospitality and professionalism from the city, in which many restaurants and bars would shut their doors early to avoid catering to the Bayou Classic's throngs.

The value of securing these potential supporters seemed so obvious to her that she found herself wondering whether past efforts had been self-defeating for a lack of confidence. "Do they not know they can ask; do they feel as though they have to have permission to ask? I don't know, why is this white woman, after some four decades, the only one that's ever asked?"

She also hit some snags. She was unsuccessful, for example, in gaining support from the Greater New Orleans Sports Foundation, a high-powered nonprofit known for its ultraconservative white membership and go-along-to-get-along blacks sitting at the table, who in her eyes were complicit in their own right. She had lobbied for the group's support, and was frustrated that she had so far failed to spark interest in the Classic. She was picking her battles carefully, though, and was reluctant to burn any bridges by complaining publicly about their lack of support. "If they can't see the opportunities of getting involved with something that can change the lives of these young people, so be it," she sniffed.

Around town, Belletto enjoyed a reputation as a turnaround artist, the go-to expert for companies, from the local United Way to the Louisiana Seafood Festival, looking to burnish their brands through wonderfully crafted and staged events. For a handsome fee, Belletto and her team essentially created or took over faltering projects, enlivened them with innovative marketing and polished execution, and trained the company's own staff to resume control. The work was rigorous but straightforward, with clients' biggest headaches typically mismanaging spending, or, rather, lavishing resources onto a grand vision and lacking realistic budgets and timelines.

Years spent behind the scenes of some of New Orleans's biggest events gave her easy access around town. It was not uncommon, for instance, for her to whisk into New Orleans's most posh restaurants through a kitchen back door, chatting up the wait staff and chef, and having a special dish sent over to her table. "I can get places where others can't," she said, matter-of-factly.

But resurrecting the Bayou Classic proved more challenging than Belletto imagined. It was more than planning parades and putting up sound and light equipment. It was fighting with potential sponsors, vendors, and everyone else to do business with the Classic as they would with any similar-sized white event. In essence, she wanted Sugar Bowl treatment for the Bayou Classic, nothing less, nothing more: just fair and equitable treatment. She wanted restaurants and bars to stay open for customers, hotels to offer reasonable rates instead of gouging, and local law enforcement to secure the streets without harassing and bullying citizens; she wanted clean zones for merchandising so that profits could be invested back into the schools. The students and families attending the Classic simply deserved a better experience than they were getting. "People have been saving up all year to come to the Bayou, and it might be the one and only trip they take," she said.

Belletto was born in North Carolina into a family of entrepreneurs and small business owners, and spent her younger years relocating a few times, to Jacksonville, Florida, and Rosedale, Michigan, before arriving in New Orleans at the age of twelve. She grew up in middle-class New Orleans east, which was then racially mixed but today is predominantly black. Her paternal grandfather owned a hardware store, along with lots of property, and Belletto's dad worked for him and later took over the business. Later he sold the assets and bought a fleet of ice-cream trucks, which successfully operated for years.

But Belletto's business and political connections can be traced directly to her mother, who worked as then mayor Marc Morial's administrative assistant, and stayed through three administrations, working fifteen years in the New Orleans City Council's office. Former mayor Moon Landrieu is credited with hiring the first African Americans into New Orleans's City Hall, which, while making him unpopular among many local whites, endeared the Landrieus to blacks for decades to come.

Growing up, the mayor's office was like a second home to Belletto—and many of the powerful leaders who came through felt like her extended family. She attributes her professional path to such an upbringing, her desire to build a business that keeps her connected to public service and governing. Her younger sister pursued a career in politics, working as an aide to Congressman Billy Tauzin and then-senator John Breaux before becoming chief of staff for U.S. congresswoman Mary Landrieu.

It was the city's current mayor, Mitch Landrieu, who suggested that Belletto bid for the Bayou Classic contract. He told her that her business was not racially diverse enough, and suggested that she start mentoring young black college students.

"I realized I had never experienced an HBCU," she said. "And that's when I put into my proposal that I would have interns from both Grambling and Southern University—and that I would take care of their housing. It's a paid internship; they do work, real work."

She also knows, though, that even her best intentions won't quiet critics who are offended that a white woman is running the state's biggest historically black college fund-raising event—and, admittedly, this fact hurts the most. "If they knew who I was, they couldn't say that," she said. "But I have to understand, and I try to understand. But they can't see that I'm different?" She joked, wryly, "Why do I have to be white? I could get so much more done. God, why didn't you give me darker skin? I'm fighting this war and that war, and I'm in the middle."

She laughed for a moment, and then she turned serious. "Look, I just want to give back and try to mitigate the hurt that a lot of people have had," she said. "If I can help some kids and they can see that some white people can be their friend, and it's not always what they imagined it to be, then that's a good thing." She threw up her hands, perhaps ready to catch all the criticism wrought by do-goodership or worse, naïveté.

John Simpson never fancied himself as militant. Growing up in the 1980s as a top student at the University of Detroit Jesuit High School and Academy, one of the city's elite high schools, John's politics were, if anything, middle-of-the-road. He spent winters skiing and summers hanging out with friends from other affluent families in Jack and Jill of America, the elite black youth social club. In fact, when the University of Michigan recruited him for its undergraduate program, he gave nary a thought to its reputation as a racially divided, often hostile environment. He was instead lured by U of M's reputation as the state's best university, that many of his brightest classmates were headed there, as well as by a bit of nostalgia. Back in the 1930s, his grandfather graduated from U of M's medical school, and in the decades since lots of his extended family had also studied there.

It wasn't long after enrolling, though, before John began regretting his decision. Having grown up in an upper-middle-class enclave of large brick colonial-style homes populated by black doctors, lawyers, and educators, John had taken for granted the inside track he had enjoyed in school and in his social life. Outgoing, smart, and handsome, with a mop of curly black hair, John never fully understood the extent of his privilege at the center of Detroit's community of young black strivers—a right anchored by a family lineage of successful and civically involved professionals. But the moment he hit U of M's campus, he watched his rather wide network of connections shrink to a tiny pool of relatively isolated black students, who made up less than 5 percent of the collegian population. If he and his buddies had once felt like big dogs, at U of M they now were reduced to blind puppies struggling to survive in a new world of some twenty-five thousand white kids dominating a campus and culture that seemed tailor made for their advancement.

John had never felt his own blackness so acutely as during his freshman year at Michigan. The cultural shift, while just forty minutes north of his home, was jarring. His roommate, a close friend from high school, was black, as was a tight-knit clan of Detroiters who had learned to survive the isolation by studying and socializing together. But all of John's professors were white, as were most of his classmates, and early on he began to feel like an interloper in his own education. "You're not part of the party," he said. "Nobody knows your name and nobody's checking for you. And you're not part of the information network; nobody's giving you the breakdown of 'take this course or that course' or 'this professor or that one.' You're there, but nobody really cares whether you succeed. You're not part of the overall university family."

John sought community within the Black Student Union and by pledging Kappa Alpha Psi, one of several black Greek organizations on campus. Joining these groups felt more natural than trying to assimilate into U of M's broader culture, especially for black nonathletes. Black athletes enjoyed a kind of sacred status at U of M, as their academic eligibility and overall happiness were important to the university's economic machinery; prized products helping to rake in millions on game day.

Despite tapping into U of M's black student community, John couldn't shake his sense of isolation. Deflating him even more were family tensions back home in Detroit. His parents had recently divorced, and John had learned midway through his freshman year that his father was remarrying. At the time, the news drove a wedge between him and his father; John wanted nothing more than to escape the family drama. The opportunity came when John's best friend and frat brother, Len Burnett, who was equally disenchanted with U of M, decided to transfer to Florida A&M University in Tallahassee. John agreed to follow. "I went to FAMU, sight unseen," he said. "Really, I was running away from a life in Michigan."

His switch to a black college prompted criticism from family and friends. He was told that only a fool would leave an elite white school like U of M for FAMU, which most major employers likely had never even heard of. The black college stigma was real and cruel: African Americans had been attending majority white institutions since the 1960s, and had since come to view black colleges as second rate. The running assumption was that those attending HBCUs were either third generation continuing a family tradition, or that they lacked the grades or financial resources to attend a mainstream university. Admittedly, back in high school, when John had received a letter offering him a full academic scholarship from FAMU, he had tossed it in the trash.

John learned quickly how wrongheaded he had been about black colleges, and in particular, FAMU, among the largest HBCUs with more than ten thousand students. His arrival instantly put him back into his social comfort zone—and sparked his professional ambition. He marveled at how quickly he swept into social circles on campus; not only brothers from Kappa Alpha Psi and countless Detroiters, but students from other parts of the country he knew—or was familiar with—from Jack and Jill. "When Lenny and I got to

FAMU, it was like we were 'made men,'" he joked. "Like under-bosses in the mob, we already knew two or three godfathers or dons at the school. People vouched for us, like 'our world is your world.' The possibility of taking that kind of cachet with you to a white university is very remote."

John and Len decided to major in business administration, which was one of FAMU's most distinguished programs, along with its school of pharmacy. John was impressed, intimidated even, by the high level of professionalism and study habits of FAMU's business school students. Instead of jeans and T-shirts, these were buttoned-down strivers who came to class coifed in navy suits and ties, and recited facts in class with almost military precision. Studying the polished look of his new classmates, John was even inspired to make over his own image; he cut off his beloved ponytail, and even ditched his earring. Meanwhile, he also bonded with the school's star pupil, Keith Clinkscales, who happened to be his fraternity brother. Clink-scales, a lanky, extraordinarily bright kid from Trumbull, Connecti-cut, was vice president of Social Labs, a role that made him an important liaison between B-school students and the corporate re-cruiters who made regular appearances on campus.

By the time John graduated in 1986, he could reflect not only on a journey of deep and enriching personal experiences and academic grinding, but also, frankly, moments of favor that had eluded his kind at U of M. There was the administrator who waived an ad-vanced course that threatened John's timely graduation; the girl-friend and TA in accounting who once bumped up one of his exam grades; and the marketing professor who once gifted him the keys to his Mercedes-Benz to sport around in during homecoming week-end. As he and his friends prepared to leave Tallahassee for the next chapter of their lives, they wept over the bittersweet transition. "When people ask me, 'What did it feel like to be at FAMU?'" he said, "I say, 'probably what it feels like to be a white dude at University of Michigan.'"

Ironically, after graduation John wound up back at the University of Michigan—at the university's law school. It was like déjà vu, sitting in lectures as his white classmates waxed smugly to approving faculty. Prior to his experience at FAMU, he would have been intimidated and perhaps even questioned his own smarts in the face of their easy command of the course work. But now he understood that his classmates likely enjoyed some edge; access to old notes, files, past exams, and inside intelligence. He worked hard to build his own personal network and support systems to ace law school, but mostly spent countless hours in the library with his head in the books. "There weren't any more hookups for me," he said. "I had to get it the old-fashioned way."

Meanwhile, he was dismayed to find many of his old friends had not yet earned their undergraduate degrees, but were still plugging away on a campus that was turning increasingly hostile to blacks. It was one of the dirty secrets of predominantly white universities: the scores of gifted black students, who, for some reason, never complete their education. A series of racially charged incidents had black students boiling; some fliers with racial epithets had been circulated around dorms; there was a sighting of a student donning a Ku Klux Klan robe; and a campus-sponsored radio broadcast had aired a segment featuring racist jokes. Upon hearing the broadcast, John was furious—and shocked that students had not mobilized to protest the racist climate at U of M. "I was like, 'We would never stand for no shit like that at FAMU,'" he said. "I was a different person by then—I was a strong, empowered black man."

John joined a group of three first-year law students and spearheaded an aggressive antidiscrimination movement at the university, sparking student protests that garnered coverage in such national publications as the *New York Times* and *Newsweek*. The protests, which galvanized black Greek organizations along with various black undergraduate and graduate students from across the campus community, even drew the attention of civil rights activist Jesse Jackson Jr. In March 1987, Jackson arrived in Ann Arbor and negotiated a six-point plan that included increased student body representation, funding for recruiting black faculty, and $35,000 annually for the Black Student Union. "That whole experience took my social awareness curve through the roof," said John, who graduated from U of M law school in 1989.

These days, John, a partner at Simpson Morton & Cross, a Detroit-based corporate law firm, still views his closest allegiance to friends and fraternity brothers from his days at FAMU—and anyone who really knows him well understands that. "We need to dispel the myth that HBCUs are second-rate institutions that blacks attend when they can't get in anywhere else," he said. "It's about more than expediency or legacy. It's about developing a sense of yourself during a critical time in your development; when the wrong influences or energy can stagger or retard your growth. I could never replace the value and trust that I gained in the time spent with these folks I met at FAMU."

Earlier this year, during the North American International Auto Show in Detroit, a local marketing executive and friend of John's organized an industry forum featuring Keith Clinkscales, who today is among the nation's highest-ranking black media executives. At fifty years old, Clinkscales has racked up a string of impressive industry feats; after leaving FAMU, he would go on, along with music mogul Quincy Jones, to birth the glossy urban music monthly *Vibe*. A decade later Clinkscales launched Vanguarde Media Inc., a portfolio of slick magazines that included *Savoy*, *Honey*, and *Heart & Soul*. More recently he has become a formidable television chief at ESPN and P. Diddy's fledgling music channel, Revolt.

But after Clinkscales's presentation, the marketing exec spirited him away to his most important meeting in Detroit: a private dinner with his buddies John and Len Burnett, the New York–based publisher of *Uptown* magazine, who was also Clinkscales's partner in building both *Vibe* and Vanguarde. Through the night, they rehashed old stories, traded some new ones, and talked a whole lot of business in between. "My friend knew it would be a mistake not to bring us together," John said. "There's no way we could be in the same city, at the same time, without connecting. That's my family."

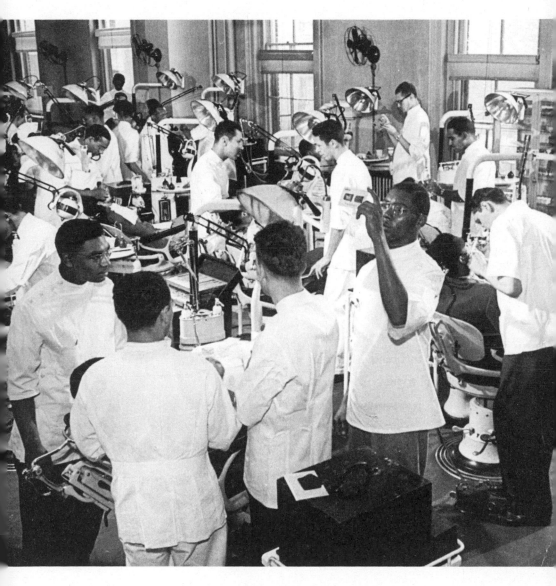

In the 1940s, dental students working in a clinic at the School of Dentistry at Howard University.

(Alfred Eisenstaedt/The LIFE Picture Collection/Getty Images)

CHAPTER 10

"WHO ARE THESE PEOPLE?"

SAVANNAH BOWEN MAY HAVE STARTED OUT her senior year as a tennis star poised to attend an elite white university, but studying under Miss Cadet-Simpkins, her English AP 12 teacher at Pelham Memorial High School in an affluent suburb outside New York City, was complicating things. The change of heart began as Miss Cadet-Simpkins, the first black teacher Savannah had ever encountered during all her years of schooling, introduced the mostly white class to Toni Morrison's *Beloved* and *For Colored Girls Who Have Considered Suicide/When the Rainbow is Enuf* by Ntozake Shange. "Those books were powerful," Savannah said. "It was the first time I had ever read a book by a black person in school. I went to class every day loving it. The other students hated it."

Actually, the awkwardness was telling when Miss Cadet-Simpkins assigned several small groups in the class to read, review, and ultimately recite various Harlem Renaissance poems. Savannah's group took on "Yet Do I Marvel" by Countee Cullen, the morose and militant sonnet that compares the most tragic characters in Greek mythology to Cullen's own lot as a black poet. When it was time for her group to recite the classic, her white colleagues froze, admitting to her that it felt uncomfortable assuming the voice of a black man and asking her to carry the load. How many white authors had Savannah been forced to recite during all her years in school, and these white kids couldn't bring themselves to read a few simple lines penned by a black man? They said they were having trouble "getting into character" for this poem. Their reticence struck her as ridiculous, and racist, but Savannah plowed ahead, reciting most of Cullen's powerful sonnet herself.

Savannah's eyes opened wider about her classmates when Miss Cadet-Simpkins scheduled an exam that they believed was untimely based on other school obligations. Savannah was accustomed to students protesting work, but in her view her classmates' pushback crossed the line into disrespect. "Everyone was being so rude to her," she said. " 'You can't do that,' they were saying, 'Are you crazy?' This was the cream of the crop of the school, not some at-risk youth, and they were being blatantly offensive to this woman. It was the tone in how they responded to her authority; that's when I realized a lot of my classmates were racists."

There were other unsettling moments. One of them occurred after the class had finished reading *For Colored Girls* and Miss Cadet-Simpkins asked students whether they believed the book was written exclusively for "colored girls" or whether there were universal themes that everyone could relate to. While Savannah could not relate directly to any of the experiences in *For Colored Girls*, the work was, at moments, cathartic to her; the rainbow of women sharing their experiences of pain and love and hardship spoke to Savannah's gut and validated her feelings of pride and power as a woman.

Unfortunately, Savannah's classmates did not share her enthusiasm for the book; in fact, her white classmates resented having to read it, even admitting they had done so only because it was required to pass the class. While Savannah admired her teacher's courage for posing the question, she loathed witnessing the Anglo-centric dialogue such a question inspired. Her peers sounded ill-informed, small-minded, and racist. "Nobody ever asked me if I could relate to Charles Dickens or Jane Eyre," she said. "Nobody had ever asked them to relate to black people. I felt like, the fact that we were even having this conversation is a symbol of your privilege in this world."

In fact, Miss Cadet-Simpkins had only fanned the flames by assigning her class to read the popular essay "White Privilege: Unpacking the Invisible Knapsack" by feminist scholar Peggy McIntosh, which, among other things, posits her belief that " . . . whites are carefully taught not to recognize white privilege, as males are taught not to recognize male privilege" and likens her racial advantage to "an invisible weightless knapsack of special provisions, maps, passports, codebooks, visas, clothes, tools, and blank checks." The essay cut hard into the attitudes and emotional predispositions that Savannah recognized in her classmates. Or as McIntosh wrote about herself: "I began to understand why we are justly seen as oppressive, even when we don't see ourselves that way. I began to count the ways in which I enjoy unearned skin privilege and have been conditioned into oblivion about its existence. My schooling gave me no training in seeing myself as an oppressor, as an unfairly advantaged person, or as a participant in a damaged culture."

Then there was Savannah's heated debate with some classmates about whether the nation's racial segregation had ended; they insisted it had, while Savannah argued that segregation persisted, pointing out that most of the workers in the school's cafeteria were Hispanic. Her classmates took offense to this, told Savannah that she was rude, and said that working in the cafeteria was good, honest labor and that it was their choice to work in the kitchen and had nothing to do with segregation. The debate dragged on through the bell and into their French class, which followed. The exchange became so heated that Savannah became emotional, breaking down in tears. "They all jumped down my throat," she said. "I was hurt. Who are these people? Who in their right mind believed this?"

A couple of days later, Miss Cadet-Simpkins took Savannah aside and privately raised the incident with her. Savannah shared that she was starting to feel alienated among her peers, and that lately she found herself wondering whether her white friends harbored racist beliefs. Miss Cadet-Simpkins calmly reassured her that her feelings were likely not altogether unwarranted, and hardly uncommon for a young girl in such social circles. The talk did not quite soothe Savannah's heartache, but having her feelings validated offered some sense of renewal.

There were other minor incidents that rubbed Savannah wrong, too. Like the boy who proclaimed that there were only "two kinds of black people: high-performing black people and low-performing, and no in between. While I'm sure he has long forgotten those words, I will never forget them." And another racially mixed boy who preferred to be called Hispanic, yet joined Savannah in accepting an award for academic achievement for black students. "I'm like, 'but he doesn't even present himself as a black man,'" she said. "I mean, I could have taken that photo op by myself."

Once, Savannah overheard a younger classmate, a racially mixed girl of Caucasian and East Indian descent, wishing for an eradication of affirmative action in education and how such policies caused teachers to look down on her and assume that she wasn't as bright as she was. Savannah, who worked on the *Pel-Mel*, the high school's newspaper, was so infuriated by the girl's stance that she wrote an editorial, essentially arguing how wrongheaded it would be to get rid of a program whose sole purpose was to help uplift minorities who have been historically disadvantaged from unfair and unjust treatment. The piece drew praise from a few administrators and faculty. Savannah's friends never mentioned it.

It was also around that time that Miss Cadet-Simpkins began encouraging Savannah to apply to her alma mater, Spelman College. Savannah, having spent most of her schooling at all-girls academies, wasn't sold on attending another. But for the first time, she began seriously thinking about her dad's alma mater, Howard University.

First Lady Michelle Obama embraces members of the Johnson C. Smith ladies' basketball team during a "Let's Move!" physical fitness promotion between games at the CIAA basketball tournament in Charlotte, N.C., on Friday, March 2, 2012. *(Nell Redmond/AP)*

CHAPTER 11

SCANDAL

THE FIRST PHONE CALL CAME ON A THURSDAY
afternoon in early June. It was from a reporter at the *Chronicle of
Higher Education*. He asked Renee Higginbotham-Brooks about the
letter she had written, and whether she really believed Howard University was in real danger of shutting down. Higginbotham-Brooks
wondered how the reporter had gotten her cell phone number. Even
more, she wondered who had leaked the letter from the Howard
trustees' portal—which, she had learned too late, was anything but
secure. Panicked, Higginbotham-Brooks stood down; she told the
reporter that the letter was intended for the board, she had no comment, and to direct his questions to the board secretary. But over the
next few hours, her phone kept ringing with calls from reporters
across the country pushing for answers.

The following day, the *Washington Post* and the *Chronicle of
Higher Education* published articles, that, to her surprise, included a
canned statement from trustee chairman Barry Rand. "Spirited debate and discourse are part of the culture of higher education," Rand
said in the statement. "The board and the university's leadership
team continue to work tirelessly to address many of the tough issues
facing colleges and universities like Howard." Citing new construction on campus, a balanced budget, and a university endowment
restored to prerecession levels, Rand assured all that the university
was strong, growing, and more competitive than ever. Board mem-

ber Stacey Mobley, too, distanced himself from Higginbotham-Brooks's letter, telling a reporter: "I have no idea where she's coming from."

Howard's council of deans, though, had written an internal memo essentially supporting Higginbotham-Brooks's view of the university's health. The letter, obtained by the *Washington Post* and published on July 1 in the newspaper, urged the ouster of Robert M. Tarola, the university's chief financial officer. The deans charged that Tarola's "fiscal mismanagement was doing irreparable harm" to Howard, and that cuts in staff based on faulty data had stymied faculty research. Meanwhile, hikes in tuition had hurt enrollment, the letter said.

Over the next few days, Higginbotham-Brooks was deluged with more press calls. She didn't answer any of them. The entire weekend, TV and radio stations and newspapers rang her home and office. Higginbotham-Brooks was, as she put it, terrified. "They were all over me," she said. "They wouldn't stop calling." She called the board secretary, pleading for help. What should she do? She was referring reporters to her, but somehow that didn't seem sufficient. Higginbotham-Brooks was told to hold tight: Judy Smith, crisis manager extraordinaire, would reach out to her next week. Yes, Judy Smith, whose notoriously shrewd Beltway spin-doctoring had inspired the character Olivia Pope on the TV show *Scandal*.

Details then become sketchy, and here's why: Howard University's bylaws stipulate that all "deliberations conducted during an executive session shall be considered confidential and may not be disclosed outside of the meeting, except as may be authorized by these Bylaws or as otherwise directed by the Chair." Such board confidentiality is further protected by additional safeguards, including this one: "minutes and other records of the Board, and of the Committees thereof, that are less than twenty-five years old are confidential and are closed for research purposes and public inspection."

The month before graduation, the board's response began. The board spent the months of April and May dealing with the letter. There were regular meetings already scheduled, but Higginbotham-Brooks said that special meetings were called leading up to the weekend of commencement. "And so we got talking points the same day we had the meeting," she said. According to Higginbotham-Brooks, Judy Smith was called in days after the letter was written but before it was leaked to the media in June.

Higginbotham-Brooks maintained that after waiting a couple of days to hear from Judy Smith, she grew impatient and called the board's general counsel for help. He advised her to issue a statement to the media acknowledging that she, in fact, authored the letter and reiterating that its contents were a matter for the university and the trustees to discuss, and that she had no further comment. Higginbotham-Brooks sent a letter saying as much to the *Washington Post*.

Constrained by board bylaws, Higginbotham-Brooks declined to discuss specifics of the proceedings. What's clear, though, based on other sources knowledgeable about the situation but who requested anonymity, is that Rand called a special meeting to deal with issues raised in Higginbotham-Brooks's letter. But not much about the letter was discussed. Instead, after an introduction by Rand, Judy Smith stepped before the board, outlining several so-called talking points for board members in the event reporters contacted them. Several trustees apparently took exception to Smith's counsel, considering her presence a distraction from the more urgent matters now facing Howard. Among the dissidents was actress and board member Debbie Allen, who told Smith that the board was more interested in getting the facts instead of spinning them. But Smith pushed ahead, performing the role for which she was hired, saying that Higginbotham-Brooks's letter was in the hands of the *Washington Post* and now posed a serious threat not only to the university's reputation, but to its finances, as Congress could move to terminate Howard's more than $220 million in federal appropriations—which would doom the university. It did not help either that Moody's was reviewing Howard's credit rating.

Many board members seemed to be blaming her for all of it, Higginbotham-Brooks says. "Barry Rand sent a note saying Moody's is coming to look at Howard 'because of the letter Renee Higginbotham wrote.' We started getting letters; students are nervous, parents are nervous and don't know whether they should send their kids to the institution 'because of the letter RB wrote.' The brand is suffering. We don't know what our enrollment is going to be, because of the letter."

It was as if an angry mob was chanting "Moody's is now here investigating us because of the press we've received because of what she did." She felt like her back was against the wall. "Like I precipitated these inquiries. Like Howard is fine but we have to fight because of her.

"And then this kid gets killed on July fourth. And they say there's a security problem at Howard and that freaks people out." According to news reports, Omar Sykes, a twenty-two-year-old Howard University senior and leader of a coed service fraternity, was shot steps away from the university's campus by a twenty-six-year-old man during an attempted robbery. A scholarship fund was started in his name.

Summer proved to be a low point for Higginbotham-Brooks— the bad news continued the next month, when a surveillance video caught the next incident. She continued, "and then in August a student gets sexually assaulted in the school of business." The student did not attend Howard, but was mentally challenged and attending a summer program.

She felt bad enough, and "then they always bring it back to some more bad press, which started with the letter."

After an intense debate over the possible fallout from Higginbotham-Brooks's letter, the board moved reluctantly to another sensitive matter: whether and how to push out President Sidney Ribeau.

Later that month, the executive committee convened in New York City for its regular meeting. It had become customary for the trustees to meet annually at the American Express headquarters in Manhattan, but there was nothing typical about this gathering. With the entrance surrounded by media, members were instructed to detour through a back entry. For the past several years, Kenneth Chenault, chief executive of Amex, would pop in to issue greetings to the board. Chenault made no such appearance this year. Higginbotham-Brooks worked to hide her nerves: the night prior, she had been warned by fellow board member Cornell Moore to prepare to be attacked. "Renee, you better have on your funeral clothes because they gonna kill you tomorrow," he told her.

Barry Rand opened the meeting. He told Higginbotham-Brooks that she would have an opportunity to speak, but then would need to recuse herself from the proceeding, as her actions would be central to the discussions. Higginbotham-Brooks kept her statement brief: she said she wrote the letter on principle alone. She said she had no other motivation. She said she loved Howard, and that she had given to Howard financially and through service over the years. Everybody in this room knows that, she said. She said she wasn't trying to be anything other than a good trustee. She also took a few shots at Judy Smith, complaining that Smith had failed to respond to her requests for counsel amid the media storm. Five days, she said, she waited for Smith to return her calls. Last, Higginbotham-Brooks challenged the board for not adhering to its own bylaws. Why do we have bylaws if we're not going to abide by them? she asked.

Higginbotham-Brooks's words drew no discernible reaction from the board. She searched their faces for some sign of support, but saw only blank stares. Then she left the room.

"When I'm called back they're talking about an ad hoc committee, but none of that happens. Howard signs another contract with Ribeau and we're on the hook for two more years. I find out about it in August after my ex-husband died." She was in disbelief. "What do you mean a contract? We voted to get rid of that man! What are you talking about we're negotiating with that man under a contract; who signed a contract?"

She questioned the protocol, and the deal itself. Although Ribeau was going to leave the presidency, his lawyers negotiated that he would remain at Howard as long as he liked. In addition to one year of his salary, he received a sabbatical and a tenured position.

There were several contenders for the presidency, but Higginbotham-Brooks did have a specific successor in mind, one who could change the view and trajectory of leadership at Howard. "I said, 'Let Dr. Frederick run this school.' That's how to regain confidence. We need to let go and let the torch pass to younger people." She continued, "Let that young man and his energy run this school. He's got the energy and passion to do it, and the intellect, and the commitment. What else do you need?"

Although there were several contenders in the running, most of the board agreed on one thing—the former mayor of Baltimore, Kurt Schmoke, was out. As one board member described him, "He is too much of an independent thinker." Nonetheless, at the moment, he and Dr. Frederick were running the school, supported by Dr. Leffall, "who has more credibility at Howard University than anybody alive today," she said.

Bill was on the line—again. Apparently, Cos wasn't quite satisfied that he had fully expressed himself a few months ago about the various social and cultural dysfunctions giving rise to the problems at black colleges—problems that, he grumbled, had only worsened since our last discussion. "We've got all these people pointing, and talking about the systemic racism," he said. "All these three-named people jumping up and talking about the man and giving power to people who don't have power."

One could easily surmise that by "three-named people," Cosby was referring to the black scholar Michael Eric Dyson, whose book, *Is Bill Cosby Right?*, harpooned Cosby's arguments as elitist and grounded in false assumptions. "Cosby's overemphasis on personal responsibility, not structural features, wrongly locates the source of poor black suffering—and by implication its remedy—in the lives of the poor," Dyson wrote in his 2005 book. "When you think the problems are personal, you think the solutions are the same. If only the poor were willing to work harder, act better, get educated, stay out of jail and parent more effectively, their problems would go away. It's hard to argue against any of these things in the abstract; in principle such suggestions sound just fine. But one could do all of these things and still be in bad shape at home, work or school."

But Cosby regarded such talk as mostly intellectual hogwash, the pabulum of poverty pimps who make their living diverting attention away from black accountability. "The only way you can reject that is, you don't want to do the work," he said. "If your Jews teach the history of who they are, whether they lost or whether they won, they know they are still trying and they are doing it correctly and they get together and have a sense of earning and education that is clear for them. And so is money. And so is health and hospitals. Jews. Black Muslims are clear: no alcohol, no drugs, no tobacco. They have signs in the neighborhood, prominent signs: 'My neighborhood, my responsibility.' The children are my responsibility."

He continued. "Now these Christian people, they got the drug dealer there. They got their little eight-year-old children who don't know what they are talking about, saying, 'I want to be a drug dealer.' Their heroes are people who dealt drugs, got shot, and turned around and stopped dealing drugs but then began to shoot out words. These people are born in the hospitals with two words that people always say: *disadvantaged*; the other word is *at-risk*. There must be some truth to it. Now, you've got these people, the excuse-ionists and the No-groes talking about I'm picking on the poor. If you tell the poor, 'Look, the way to get out of this is to stay on your child, stay on your parenting, even if you're separated. Make sure you give information to your child that will keep them out of harm's way. Don't let your children eat the wrong food. Don't let your children go to places where they are going to be attacked. These children need to be told about their history, told about the value and the beauty of reading, writing, and math.'"

Many of Cosby's arguments about what plagued America's black colleges were spot on. For example, Cosby believed Howard was still a leader among HBCUs, yet suffered from its top administrators' denial of the struggles it's facing. "There's nothing wrong with that university except the broken spirit and glazed eyes of those people on that board, and the lies that they are living and telling each other," he said.

Cosby insisted that what Howard needed most was a forensic audit to track where its money was being spent, or rather where its abuses were occurring. He wanted to see signatures on checks, to put names and faces on what he called the "duplicitousness" occurring at America's black colleges. "Look at the damage that can be done while people are standing around using an egregious reason like 'We don't want people to know.' This is tantamount to 'We don't want people to know we have dirty laundry.' Well, it keeps piling up and the stench is horrible and people are getting sick from it. And the students deserve better, the professors deserve better."

By now, evidence of double-dealing at HBCUs was certainly piling up. For months, there had been reports of corruption at Alabama State University, which had stumbled its way through a forensic audit that, in the end, alleged fraud, conflict of interest, and abuse of public funds by members of the university's board of trustees, including its chairman and vice chairman. The state legislature had ordered the audit and the final report, which dominated the headlines for weeks, painting an embarrassing portrait of Alabama State as a cesspool of fraud, nepotism, and financial waste. There were contracts with no deliverables amounting to more than $2.5 million—some to board family members. One instance involved a board member who, along with his son and daughter-and-law, ran a sports foundation and raked in $864,000 from the university between 2007 and 2013 with nary a contract with ASU. When Dr. Joseph Silver, the university's president, began nosing around asking questions about the practices, the board fired him. But Silver, like a character in some dime-store crime novel, dropped a box of damning financial documents on the governor's doorstep on his way out of office.

There were other instances of HBCU wrongdoing, too. Dr. Christopher Brown, who Alcorn State University, in Mississippi, once hailed as a transformational leader, went down after whistleblowers exposed his purchasing violations involving more than $795,000. Among other things, the probe unearthed renovations at the president's house that were secured without bids, a violation of the state's procurement laws. His aide, meanwhile, was collecting fees from the university tied to another business employing him on the side, as well as spending bond money not authorized in the loan agreement. The investigations by Mississippi's college board and ethics commission of unlawful spending forced Brown and two others to resign, although it was unclear for some of the allegations whether Brown was aware that the expenditures violated contracts or law.

At South Carolina State University, the FBI levied federal corruption charges against the university's board chairman, Jonathan

Pinson, and its university police chief, Michael Bartley, for kick-backs on a 120-acre land deal. Wiretaps of their cell phones uncovered the $3 million land sale, and that Pinson was angling for a Porsche Cayenne valued at $110,000 and Bartley some $30,000 in cash and a new all-terrain vehicle. Instead, Bartley, who pled guilty, faced up to five years in prison, and Pinson faced up to twenty-five years and a $250,000 fine. Among the corruption charges was $60,000 in kickbacks to Pinson for homecoming events from an entertainment company in which he was a business partner.

And then there was the infamous Paine Project, a website specifically created as a rallying cry for those students, faculty, staff, and alumni calling for the ouster of Paine College's current president, George C. Bradley. The allegations in this case were lurid, including Bradley's use of U.S. Department of Education Title III funds to pay child support to a former student, and that, among other things, the board of trustees under Bradley's leadership used nearly half of the university's $8.2 million endowment as collateral to a line of credit. The activities triggered concerns of financial instability by the Southern Association of Colleges and Schools Commission on Colleges, an accrediting body for colleges and universities, and resulted in the college being put on probation status for ten standard violations.

Even if Howard's woes paled against those of various other HBCUs, it was hard to overlook, for instance, the questionable bonuses Dr. Ribeau had awarded—$1.1 million in bonuses to senior managers at the university. The payments struck a harsh chord among students and faculty alike, as the university was suffering furloughs as well as physical deterioration of classrooms and dorms;

there were students reporting sightings of rats and roaches. The bonuses only reaffirmed Cosby's characterization of many HBCU leaders as duplicitous, extolling platitudes of educating the next generation while perpetrating actions that were nothing less than destructive to the students who trusted them with their future—and money. "When Howard's trustees point to Renee, it's the same as a crucifixion. They want to crucify this woman who did not slip the information to anybody. She wrote a letter as opposed to standing there and telling these people. Renee's letter is not the problem. The problem is the people who are still supporting the people behind this mess."

Members of Wilberforce University's Delta Sigma Theta
Sorority lean back in unity at a 2013 march in Washington,
D.C., that retraced the footsteps of the organization's
founders, who participated in the women's suffrage march
a century before.

(Marvin Joseph/The Washington Post via Getty Images)

CHAPTER 12

THE WAR AT WILBERFORCE

SOME FIVE HUNDRED MILES AWAY FROM THE bustle of New York City, in the flat midwestern cow-pasture town just outside of Xenia, Ohio, Dr. Patricia Hardaway, president of Wilberforce University, had begun to surrender. Even if she had not verbally resigned, her actions—she had begun retreating into her office for hours at a time—foretold a sense of doom. Hardaway, at sixty-two years old, had not yet given serious thought to what she might do next in her career. Still, she knew it was just a matter of time before the trustees at Wilberforce sent her packing, or forced her to resign; that either way, the chaos swirling around her—student protests, restive faculty, plummeting enrollment—would eventually carry her out of there.

Settling into such a fate was tough; it hurt accepting the fact that Richard Deering, a scruffy old white economics professor who she felt fancied himself as a kind of kingpin at Wilberforce, had actually gotten the best of her. The more she talked about it, the angrier she became. The entire university culture reminded her, regrettably, of a Deep South plantation in which a white man lords over a bunch of house and field Negroes. "He has used this university, since 1968— when I was a student here and when he came on as a professor—as his plantation. He sees himself as a massa."

Frankly, it was astounding that a university president was resorting to plantation analogies to explain her management troubles.

"I am serious. That's how he sees this. And over the decades he has obstructed change for the better, he has manipulated students and the faculty like his Miss Kizzies and Chicken Georges." Deering did not specifically address Hardaway's characterizations or accusations, but acknowledged there was bad blood between them.

The irony in all this was that Hardaway, a Wilberforce alum who rose to become a powerful New York corporate attorney, was installed in 2008 as a kind of antidote to the rocky tenure of the university's former president Floyd Flake. Also an alum, Flake was a former U.S. congressman and pastor of the large Greater Allen A.M.E. Cathedral in Queens, New York. The board had tapped Flake six years prior, figuring that a high-profile leader with a Rolodex of well-heeled connections could breathe new life into Wilberforce, which boasted the distinction as the nation's first black college to be owned and operated by African Americans, founded in 1856. But Flake's tenure ended in turmoil—a faculty complaint to the state Attorney General's Office alleged he plundered the university for personal gain—and his bitter resignation.

When Hardaway, a board member, was asked to take the reins in lieu of a proper search, she obliged. The search never occurred, and Hardaway had inherited more problems than she could solve within a reasonable time frame. Enrollment was sliding fast, campus buildings were in dire need of repair (students complained of fungus on dormitory walls), faculty hadn't received raises in years, and alumni support of the university had bottomed out.

Hardaway happened to be among several HBCU presidents losing leadership stripes. The thud of leaders tumbling out of black college offices was loud. It was of little consolation that Barack Obama, America's first black president, had just a few months before taken his oath of office for a second term on a bible once owned by Dr. Martin Luther King, a Morehouse grad. The reality was that HBCU corner offices had morphed into a kind of revolving door, as some twenty permanent HBCU presidencies were either vacant or inhabited by some new recruit. Even worse, several presidents got the boot before even finishing out their first contract, while others abruptly threw in the towel or were pushed out by boards that had lost confidence in them.

The wreckage included veterans David Wilson, president of Morgan State University, and Joseph Silver, president of Alabama State University, both public HBCUs. Wilson, who had served two years at Morgan State's helm, was looking forward to renewing his contract that summer, while Silver was jettisoned after about two months on the job. At Shaw University in North Carolina, Irma McClaurin, the university's third president in three years, called it quits after eleven months on the job.

Over the next couple of months, there would be other empty seats: By October, Dr. Gilbert L. Rochon, who had served three years as president of Tuskegee University, would resign his role, and Dr. Matthew Jenkins would take over as interim president. Stillman College president Ernest McNealey, who had served since 1997, was ousted by the university's trustees, who cited sagging enrollment, poor employee morale, and high turnover, as well as strained ties to the business community as reasons for the decision. Norfolk State University's president Dr. Tony Atwater was abruptly fired, too, by the board, after two years on the job following poor marks by the university's accrediting agency. This was on top of all the vacancies closing out the previous year at Alabama State, Arkansas at Pine Bluff, Bennett, Bethune-Cookman, Coppin State, Florida A&M,

Lincoln University of Missouri, Mississippi Valley State, North Carolina Central, Shaw, and South Carolina State.

If such instability in the HBCU executive suite was unprecedented, it also reaffirmed suspicions that many black colleges not only were losing their way, but lacked a fresh vision for getting back on course. The result was that the days when HBCU presidents enjoyed long, cushy tenures were over; these days, they were expected to hit the ground running, schmoozing the business community for financial support, all the while pursuing bold strategies that bolstered graduation and retention rates, as well as attracting a new crop of talented students.

As NAACP president Benjamin Todd Jealous put it in an open letter after Saint Paul's College announced that it was shutting its doors: "Like many HBCUs, the college lacked a wealthy donor base or strong endowment that could help it weather the financial storm," Jealous wrote. " . . . Saint Paul's demise should serve as a wake-up call to those who care about the future of HBCUs."

In keeping with Jealous's analogy, Hardaway really never had time to even set the clock. The moment she took over at Wilberforce, she came up against Deering, president of the university's faculty association. Much of his power derived from being on the front lines when the faculty unionized, during which many without a master's degree or Ph.D., including Deering (who has an M.S. but not a Ph.D.), were awarded tenure review based on, among other things, years of service. Deering had freer rein under former president Dr. John L. Henderson and was amicable with Flake, but clashed almost instantly with Hardaway.

Actually, the bad blood between Hardaway and Deering started before she took over as president. Flake had appointed Hardaway provost during his final days. But when Flake's vice president at the time negotiated a new labor contract with the union, Hardaway thought the process was being mismanaged and asked to step in. Deering rubbed her the wrong way—as a know-it-all bully. "When one talks to him, it's a soliloquy followed by a monologue, and then he becomes the epilogue and the chorus," she said, sighing. "And it was a waste of time. They were spending hours upon hours getting nowhere."

For his part, Deering viewed himself as a kind of guardian of Wilberforce, a seasoned academic with enough backbone and institutional clout to prevent Hardaway from dragging down the university even further than her predecessor. He worried that without his intervention, Wilberforce might go the way of Morris Brown, which got into trouble because the school mismanaged its federal financial aid, or Barber-Scotia, which hit hard times due to alleged academic misconduct, or Paul Quinn because of declining enrollment.

Deering was sentimental about his time at Wilberforce. He arrived at the university in 1968, proud to join a tradition that included such stalwarts as opera singer Leontyne Price, sociologist William Julius Wilson, and W. E. B. Du Bois, a former professor at the university. He had attended Carroll College in Wisconsin for his undergraduate degree, then, for graduate school, the University of Illinois at Champaign. From 1981 to 1991, Deering served as division chair for the department of economics, when Wilberforce's total enrollment was over one thousand students. The fact that he rose to such heights without earning his doctoral degree was something of a sensitive topic for him—an embarrassment, frankly—and put him on the defensive against more credentialed colleagues. He shrugged off the lack of a Ph.D. as status quo at a small liberal arts college like Wilberforce. "For most of Wilberforce's history it never really mattered," he explained to me.

Now Wilberforce was dying, and by his estimation had a year to turn things around—something Hardaway was clearly not capable of. Her performance was atrocious; that fall, only 75 freshmen had matriculated. The number had been 167 the previous year. Back in 2007, 250 enrolled. Even the board, which just two years ago was a solid supporter of Hardaway, had recently called a special meeting about the pitiful numbers. He figured they were ready to pull the plug on Hardaway.

In fairness, Hardaway's biggest problem was the crushing debt she had inherited. The university had recently built two new dorms: Henderson Hall in 2000 and the Living Learning Center in 2007. The problem was the debt load Wilberforce incurred building those dorms: $6 million on the first and $7 million for the other. The university borrowed to cover the contract, issuing new bonds and refinancing lots of other debt. In all, the university issued about $22 million in new debt in 2007.

Hardaway was able to refinance about $24 million to ward off default. But this also required deep cuts: she implemented a new budget that called for salary reductions at 15 percent for herself and senior team members, and 5 percent for nonunion workers. She sliced about a million dollars out of operating costs. There was also eleven weeks of furlough for all employees, starting in December 2008.

Resistance was strong. The university's choir director was so infuriated by the slashing that he quit and took his formidable talents to Central State, taking more than half the choir with him. That previous fall, hundreds of students held a demonstration in front of the main administration building. Students threatened to transfer to Central State.

"She wouldn't even talk to them," Deering sniffed. "She just stood up there in the Wolfe Building looking down at people.

"She doesn't have the personality to sit down and talk to people, whether it's faculty or alumni or contributors, board members or students. She doesn't have the personality to talk to people with differing opinions."

In her own defense, Hardaway also pointed to student demonstrations, which had become an all-too-regular occurrence. One year students were congregating in the lobby of the Wolfe Administrative Building, which houses the president's office. Hardaway had heard Deering was the instigator. Instead of taking a defensive posture with students, she disarmed her critics by inviting students into her office for a civil, behind-closed-doors discussion.

Recent reports of a foreign military conflict came to mind when she described Deering's strategy. "They would put the children and civilians on the front lines so the Americans wouldn't fire on them. He puts the students out there because he knows that we're not going to suspend students for demonstrating."

But the demonstrations over the choir director's resignation constituted a different situation in her mind. She refused to talk, she said, "because these were faculty issues, and not student-related." She clarified that she was "not going to discuss faculty issues with students. And vice versa."

The fix for that debt problem, many said, was a merger between Wilberforce and Central State, but there has been bad blood between the schools dating back to the mid-1940s, when the state tried to take over the school. There were property disputes; the state claimed it owned the land. Documents were stolen, preventing students from getting their records. Students accepted into Wilberforce would get off the train in Xenia and be sent to Central State. "The history is contentious," said Hardaway.

History aside, tensions were still running high at Wilberforce. Says Deering: "Am I the troublemaker at Wilberforce or is Pat Hardaway the troublemaker? What has she brought to the institution? She wants to be mad with the messenger instead of the message. We need to be dealing with issues instead of sweeping them under the rug. It's got to stop."

In late September, Moody's Investors Service issued the headline: "Moody's Downgrades Howard's Credit." Moody's early July review of Howard's books resulted in "Howard University Issue of the District of Columbia Revenue Bonds being downgraded from A3 to BAA1," fancy talk for a serious drop in confidence among the university's investors. Although Moody's acknowledged Howard University's strong brand, it cited several challenges, including the Howard University Hospital revenue shortfalls, declining enrollment, and budget cuts.

Since 1868, Howard University had owned and operated a teaching hospital serving its immediate community. Recently, the university had been subsidizing the medical center's operations, as it faced a $17 million operational shortfall in 2013. At the top of the downward spiral were the aging facilities needing improvement. The low-quality facilities impeded top-notch physician recruitment, resulting in a hospital that was unfit to aggressively compete in the health care marketplace. Compounding the problem was the hospital's dependence on Medicaid, which instituted a new system that increased competition among providers to attract and retain patients. These factors had led to declining patient volume. If leadership was unable to sell the hospital, develop a joint venture to keep the hospital alive, or outsource to improve management of the hospital, it would have to agree on an alternative plan of action, which would likely involve closing the hospital's doors.

School enrollment numbers had also declined some 6 percent, and most of that reduction was a result of increased criteria for families to qualify for the federal Direct PLUS loans. While some families successfully appealed their loan denial, the damage had already been done, and Howard was unable to recover and enroll all of those students again.

The university achieved a positive bottom line for its operations, but this was due to what analysts called "nonrecurring financial solutions," essentially short-term fixes to mask a bad situation. Because the university depended on federal income for one quarter of its revenue, it was especially vulnerable to budget cuts and the sporadic nature of payments from the federal government. Fund-raising efforts did not yield strong results, either. That the university's liquidity depended on a $135 million credit agreement set to expire in mid-2014 was a factor in the downgrade as well. Adding to the situation was the historical disagreement between the Howard community and its board members in making financial decisions, one that had already resulted in delays in reducing expenses. "Management estimates that the university is behind budget for the first three months of the fiscal year," Moody's reported.

Alabama State University linebacker Leland Baker (50) and the university's head coach celebrate a turnover in the 2013 victory against Alabama A&M University in the Magic City Classic.

(*Michael Wade/Icon SMI/Corbis*)

CHAPTER 13

MAGIC CITY

GENE HALLMAN, ONE OF ALABAMA'S TOP SPORTS marketing gurus, was sitting in his suburban Birmingham office imagining the largest wobble dance in history. The wobble was a popular, rhythmic group dance—or line dance as it is called—generally associated with weddings, family reunions, and other festive gatherings. Much like its electric slide predecessor, the wobble was also synonymous with black culture, inspired, as it was, from the rapper V.I.C.'s bass-heavy hit "Wobble Baby."

But such music trivia pulled few heartstrings for Hallman, a middle-aged white guy far more familiar with waggling over golf balls than wobbling to rap beats. Hallman was a straight-ahead event promoter whose company, Bruno Event Team, was known for creating some of the region's highest-profile sporting events, from the PGA's BMW Championship to the Honda Indy Grand Prix of Alabama to University of Alabama football games. For the past several months he had been brainstorming ways to set new attendance and revenue records at the Magic City Classic, Alabama's most popular football game, pitting Alabama A&M University against Alabama State University. He believed creating a wobble line that made it into *Guinness World Records*—Legion Field holds nearly seventy-two thousand fans—would be a big step in that direction.

There was no disputing that in the insular, chest-thumping world of black colleges, the Magic City Classic had become a bona fide crown jewel, beloved as much for its longstanding roots as its soulful energy. The gridiron showdown between Alabama A&M University and Alabama State University was legendary, dating back to 1924 (when Alabama State won 30–0), and becoming even hotter in 1946 when the teams broke the color line and began playing at Birmingham's Legion Field.

There are, of course, many great HBCU football weekends; among them are Howard University's homecoming weekend, the Bayou Classic in New Orleans, and North Carolina A&T's homecoming in Greensboro. It's likely that somewhere, at this very moment, black college loyalists are debating which HBCU hosts the best homecoming or football classic, comparing everything from Greek step shows, to nightlife options, to the draw of big-name performers.

Yet even among these popular gatherings, Magic City had grown to occupy a revered place in the annual roster of HBCU events. Some of its mystique was simply due to setting, as Birmingham is a trove of painful and triumphant moments within our nation's civil rights narrative; among them Dr. King's famous letter from a jail cell, and the four little girls who died in the bombing of a local Baptist church. This modern jamboree in the Deep South brought a sense of reclamation, a real homecoming of sorts for black northerners who relished sliding into their southern drawl over plates of barbecued ribs and corn bread. There was, too, the hard reality that even today Birmingham's black residents are disproportionately lower income, and for all their troubles bring a diehard's passion to the colossal tailgating parties—a constellation of family reunion–like gatherings circling Legion Field and spilling out into the nearby neighborhoods for three straight days and nights.

But as much as the event felt at moments almost spiritual, Hallman understood more than most that the Magic City Classic represented big business. Each year, the event brought in more than $20 million in revenue to the city's hotels, restaurants, bars, and nightclubs. And ticket sales to the game raked in $450,000 for both universities. The largest Magic City Classic, in 2011, lured sixty-six thousand fans. As Hallman put it: "Universities across this country are being impacted by the steady decline in public funding; I'm not commenting on whether that decline is warranted or not. I'm just saying it's a new day, a new reality, and if you're not a big university with a big, thriving athletic department like Alabama or Florida, the world of college athletics continues to change, and the gap is becoming wider between the haves and have-nots. For HBCUs, that puts pressure on classics like Magic City to continue to pump money into those athletic departments."

Hallman estimated that the annual football game netted about a half-million dollars per year for each school, after expenses. Sure, the schools got a cut from the NCAA basketball tournament because the Southwestern Athletic Conference, or SWAC, always sends its champion to that big tourney, and each college in the conference gets a piece of the revenue. But those dollars paled in comparison to that half million per year Alabama A&M and Alabama State bring in from Magic City, which stands as the schools' largest single line item of revenue for their athletic departments. Just a couple of weeks before, Hallman was walking across the Alabama A&M campus with a university official who was proudly pointing out various capital projects, from dorms to administration buildings, punctuating each sight of new brick and mortar with the chorus: "Magic City paid for that."

Hallman's Bruno took over promoting Magic City in 2000 after a series of less-than-desired performances by other firms, many of which were black owned and had scant resources to invest in the event to maximize the bounty for schools. He conceded to me that initially he felt some reluctance vying to become the point man for the state's biggest black tradition. "We weren't sure what kind of reception we'd get," Hallman recalled. "Here's this white guy coming and saying, I want to run this. I'll never forget the first meeting I had. Dr. John Knight, who is the chief operating officer of Alabama State University, told me, 'Don't worry about the black and white issue—this is about green.' He said we've not been able to monetize these games for our universities the way we need to."

Since then, Hallman had found a winning strategy for Magic City: smart politics, big celebrities, and easy access. The three-part formula was, in his eyes, the best antidote for luring a younger demographic to games to replenish the pool of aging, less active core customers, a trend affecting not just HBCUs but all sporting events. The fact was, younger crowds were finicky. He learned as much promoting the University of Alabama, which was having trouble filling the stands even giving away tickets. In researching their lack of interest, Hallman found that the number one reason students stayed away from games was that their social media didn't work in the stadium; the crowd weakened cell phone signals. "So we've got a whole new paradigm coming," Hallman said. "How do we get this twenty-five-year-old hooked on the Magic City Classic, continue to attend for years to come, and make it part of an annual tradition?"

These days, Classic promoters needed deep pockets—not just their own but government and business as well. If previous Magic

City promoters were criticized for lacking strong ties to local and national powerbrokers, Hallman proved otherwise. He persuaded Birmingham's mayor to take a greater stake in the annual financial boon to the city's businesses. The city now pumps more than a half-million dollars into the Classic, and has also worked with Bruno to develop a smooth shuttle system that enables older fans to park downtown and hop on a bus to Legion Field so they don't have to deal with the traffic jams. Even more, they sold such corporations as Coke, State Farm, and Coors Light on everything from sponsorships to skyboxes.

The weekend's glamour quotient has also risen under Hallman. When Bruno took over, the only stars around were in the night sky. But his team hatched the concept of bringing a celebrity ambassador to the game—a luminary from the sports or entertainment world that made a halftime appearance on the field to add some sizzle to festivities. The first ambassador was home run king Willie Mays, a choice Hallman sheepishly admits wasn't exactly drawn from consensus. Mays was his childhood hero. "Yeah, I did that more for myself than anyone else," he said, chuckling. Since then, the ambassador roster has included Magic Johnson, Charles Barkley, LL Cool J, Lisa Raye, Wendy Williams, and Tom Joyner. This year it was Ice Cube. The pizzazz possesses its own kind of gravity: black entertainers throughout the region make appearances and even perform at the myriad ancillary events throughout the Classic, whether it's pep rallies, corporate kickoffs, or various independent parties that pop up across town. Some years are better than others, Hallman said, as the ambassador selection process is anything but scientific. "Here's how we pick 'em: Who's big and available?"

He added: "Look, I haven't always been the most accurate judge of who is going to be the best ambassador, obviously, because I'm white, and don't know who the crowds will go crazy over. I'm thrilled that we got Cube this year. He's really big. We got him through MillerCoors. They are making a big push into the African American market. So they jumped all over it and helped us pull him in."

Still, Hallman faced serious challenges. While the coveted twenty-five-year-old demographic was now hanging out at the Magic City festivities, only a portion was actually attending the football game. "They are taking part in the social atmosphere, which is wonderful, but we gotta figure out a way to get them in the game. The time to look is a few minutes before halftime to truly know the attendance. Every year we are about ten or twelve thousand short of selling it out. We can't get over the hump. And we've got to get there."

Hallman had an idea for this, too, but knew it would spark outrage. To encourage folks to go to the game, he was considering securing the side west of Legion Field, the hub of tailgating, and allowing only those into that area who had a game ticket. The east side of the stadium would still be open to people without tickets. Magic City veterans, accustomed to moving freely through the grounds, would likely protest such a radical change. "But we're getting to the point where if you're going to come and park in that area and stress our traffic and parking capabilities, you need to buy a ticket," he said. "Don't load up your car and park and just walk around the stadium and hang out. And then hang out in the evening and then go somewhere else. We need you to come into the game. Sure, some folks will be upset. I'll take the bullets because at the end of the day, if it's about making more money for the universities, so be it."

Ultimately, though, it'll take more than successful football weekends to keep HBCUs alive. It'll take strong and consistent leadership, and bringing an end to a culture of brutal politics causing a revolving door in senior roles. "We've done the Classic for thirteen years, and in that thirteen years we have dealt with approximately twenty different presidents and athletic directors between the two institutions. So, it's not just money that's a problem. It's power, and other things. Look, the politics will kill the HBCUs before any of the other stuff."

Later that morning, Dr. George French, the president of Miles College in Birmingham, Alabama, walked across a decidedly energized campus. Cranes and trucks and work crews obstructed nearly every sight line as construction of new buildings took shape across the landscape. "Some schools are stuck on academics," said French, a Miles College alum. "But we need to have institutional advancement to get that money, and develop these campuses. We have to give folks something to look at."

French swept an arm wide across the landscape to show off the Miles panorama. "Now, folks will give to this," he said proudly.

During the university's most recent capital campaign, Miles raised $42 million to improve the campus infrastructure, which included building a new 204-bed residence hall, a dining hall, and a student activities center, as well as the stately white colonial-style admissions center. "This is my new trustee board room," he said, as he whisked through the facility, which was still under construction. "Right now we have a very small room that we meet in. But this seats twenty-six members."

He paused in the atrium. "We can host some nice receptions here. Back here is where the admissions office will be." And he continued into a private area toward the rear of the building. "This is the legacy room where we show pictures all the way back from 1898. It's also where we interview students for admission."

Striding into the center of the room, he said, "I set this up to look like home because some of the students will not have come from homes that look like that, or a living room that looks like that, so I want them to aspire to something they've never had.

"We're doing this methodically and deliberately. I want our students to have the best of the best. I want them to be used to the finer things in life, become spoiled with the finer things in life, so that they graduate and go out there and become successful."

French, an ordained Christian Methodist Episcopal minister, went on to say that Miles's transformation was a blessing borne of patience during tough economic times. "What we've been able to do through the glory of God, is that while the economy was tanking, we purchased what is now the north campus four years ago, where there was a four-hundred-thousand-square-foot hospital. The question was, what do you do with a hospital? How do you pay for this property? How do you demolish a hospital? They said it would be three million dollars to demolish. We waited until the economy tanked, and because we were in such a strong financial position, with positive cash flow, we went back, and they dropped the price to 1.4 million dollars. We saved 1.6 million dollars because we were fluid and liquid when the economy was down."

Instead of complaining about waning government support, French has remained the optimist, and he has avoided the negative effects of changes in credit standards of the Direct PLUS Loan program. His students typically hailed from such poor families, they didn't qualify for Direct PLUS loans even under the old standard. "Some of my colleagues had an average student gap of seven thousand dollars," he said, referring to other black college presidents. "My average student gap was fifteen hundred dollars, so it was manageable." Miles was able to close the gap through alumni chapters donating grants, scholarships, and other financial gifts.

These days, French had his eye on amassing more land around the university, which included a tough 140-unit low-rise public housing project. "What we now need to do is acquire the housing projects that separate this campus from the north campus," he said. "That will allow us to combine and double the size of our campus."

He paused, dreamily, and then continued laying out his grand plans. "Did I mention that we were approved for a radio station? We launched WMWI some years ago, but it has a paltry wattage. But we just got FCC approval for one hundred thousand watts. That's right, we will be the only jazz radio station in Birmingham, Alabama—right here at Miles College."

A Southern University marching band drum major gets
the crowd going before their halftime performance in a
2005 football game against Grambling State University.
(*Bob Levey/WireImage for AOL*)

CHAPTER 14

A WOLF BY THE EAR

DR. NORMAN FRANCIS, THE EIGHTY-FOUR-YEAR-
old president of Xavier University of Louisiana and black college
patriarch, had grown all too familiar with all the apocalyptic talk
surrounding HBCUs—the worries over funding, criticism about
leadership, fretting over student performance, and predictions generally that black colleges were nearing their deathbed. Francis also
understood that in the increasingly volatile world of HBCUs, he was
the rare exception, a black college president with a sustained and
impressive track record at a single university that spanned a couple
of generations. He was thirty-seven years old when he took the reins
of Xavier and, through God's grace, had weathered enough dooms-
days to become the nation's longest-serving college president, black
and white alike. The extraordinarily long tenure had taught Francis
quite a bit, but learning to maintain his composure—and
optimism—during even the roughest times had proved his most
valuable lesson. "A month after I was appointed president forty-five
years ago, I was asked this question, 'Are black colleges still relevant?' And I still get that question all the time."

Francis, caramel in complexion with wavy graying hair, chuckled
and leaned in conspiratorially. "It's a question that has no real valid answer because we are no different than any other institution in the United
States," he said. "We are all struggling, and yet we will all survive to the
extent that this country needs us. There will be white schools, small

schools that are going to drop off the wagon. Surely, we've already had black schools of long standing that have not been able to make it. But are black schools going to be wiped off the map? Won't happen."

He was sitting at a large oval conference table in a cavernous meeting room adorned with a picturesque view of campus—a landscape that not that long ago was drowning under several feet of water dumped by Hurricane Katrina. That disaster back in 2005 may have crippled the campus for nearly five months, but Francis had managed to keep Xavier moving forward—with the help, of course, of millions in FEMA funds, lots of borrowed money, and the grit of Xavier's faculty and staff. "I can't tell you what it takes to bring a school back when you are closed for a whole semester," he said. "We had water damage to every building."

Francis stood and stepped over to the window, pointing northeast across campus to a new stately chapel looming in the distance. St. Katharine Drexel Chapel, a $10 million structure, makes a bold statement about Xavier's vitality, especially to commuters traveling along New Orleans's Pontchartrain Expressway. Designed by famous architect César Pelli, the stone, octagon-shaped chapel topped with a copper roof boasts distinction as Pelli's first foray into church design during a career of skyscrapers. Francis built the chapel to honor Saint Katharine Drexel, a nun and heiress who founded the university in 1925.

"Our founder, who is now a saint in the Catholic Church and whose father was a Drexel alumnus, gave up all of her money to become a nun and open up high schools on the Navajo reservations and in the South. She opened only one university, Xavier. When she died in 1955, all the funding was cut off. So we have had a hard time raising money because people figure Xavier's still got all this money. And that's not true."

Francis grew up dirt poor in Lafayette, Louisiana, one of five children born to a barber at the end of the Great Depression. Francis began pulling his weight early on, finding work as a youngster milking cows. During high school, he impressed one of his teachers enough that she recommended him to Xavier, and he went on a work scholarship, toiling four years in the university library mending damaged books. He went on to study law at Loyola University, in 1955 becoming the law school's first black graduate. In 1957 he joined Xavier as dean of men and eleven years later was appointed president. Since then, Francis has devoted much of his energy to building Xavier's legacy in the life sciences, specifically pharmacology. Along with Howard University, Xavier's College of Pharmacy, founded in 1927, remains one of only two black colleges of pharmacy in the nation. In life science curriculums, the university continually boasts a high ranking compared to other U.S. institutions. "You can't walk into a drugstore in Louisiana and not meet a Xavier graduate, whether that graduate is black, white, or Vietnamese," he said.

In his view, the future of all American universities, not just HBCUs, rests in their ability to turn out graduates with backgrounds in science, technology, engineering, and math, the STEM subjects. Unfortunately, there was mounting evidence that the U.S. was sorely lagging in these fields. Just weeks ago, the Organisation for Economic Co-operation and Development had surveyed more than 150,000 people age 16 to 65 in 24 different countries, and found that the United States ranked 21 out of 23 countries in math and 17 out of 19 countries in problem solving. For African Americans, the situation was especially dire: while blacks account for 12 percent of the U.S. population, and 11 percent of all students beyond high school, they earned a paltry 7 percent of all STEM bachelor's degrees, 4 percent of master's, and 2 percent of P.hD.s, according to the National Center for Education Statistics.

Francis had been exploring the issue of academic competitiveness for years, in the southeast region as well as nationally. In the '80s, he was selected as a committee member to study the nation's public school crisis. The result was the publication of the seminal study *A Nation at Risk*, which at the time set new standards for high schools. "I could have written that report," he said. "I had seen the demise of school systems in the seventies and the effect on black youngsters." Ironically, Francis said President Reagan's motivation for convening the committee was the growing spectacle of illiterate white children. He recalled this quote from the report: "If an unfriendly foreign power had attempted to impose on America the mediocre educational performance that exists today, we might well have viewed it as an act of war."

At Xavier, he said, he had worked hard to make the curriculum transformative for students. If the majority of students arrived underprepared to perform at the college level, they graduate and progress beyond expectations. "In America today, where are the black Ph.D.s coming from: Harvard, Yale, and all that? No, the highest number and percentage who are getting Ph.D.s at the Harvards or the Yales are coming from black schools," he said. "The National Science Foundation recently published a report on undergraduate schools who graduate the most Ph.Ds. Xavier is number one in life science Ph.D.s and number five in biological Ph.D.s. And Xavier is number one in graduating young people getting undergraduate degrees in the physical and biological sciences. That shouldn't be—we are too small to be having the number one place on the undergraduate side. But were we not producing these folks, where would black Americans who are being sought after by these major institutions be?"

There was a time when Dr. Ron Mason, now president of Southern University, had spoken to Norman Francis about working under him at Xavier, but Francis wasn't interested in an understudy shadowing him. Or gunning for him. It may be a good thing, as Mason has moved on to become among the most progressive thinkers in the black college space. Consider his Five-Fifths Agenda, a program he is piloting at Southern's Honoré Center and which he hopes to replicate across the country.

The program was inspired during a dinner conversation with his friend and colleague Susan Taylor Batten, head of the Association of Black Foundation Executives. Throughout the evening, Mason and Batten jousted over the problems facing young black men and all the economic issues adding fuel to the fire. Everyone claimed to have the solution, Batten said, yet there was nobody out there actually doing anything.

"So I went home that night and put together this program called the Five-Fifths Agenda for America."

The idea involves recruiting black males from public schools, educating them at Southern on full scholarships, and after graduation employing them as teachers back at their local high schools. In Mason's view, the program would serve as a new value proposition for HBCUs and at the same time reclaim the human capital of troubled black males. The program, rooted in Mason's perspectives on American history and labor, was also shaped by his background running the business side of Tulane for nearly two decades.

"The American Revolution was about money," he said one afternoon, sitting in his office in Baton Rouge, where the main campus of Southern University's collegiate system is located. "Rich guys on this side of the ocean left because their business partners on the other side of the ocean were taxing them too much. They decided to fight this fight by setting up their own economic base and they called it America. They had certain principles in mind when they designed this country: truth, justice, of the people by the people. But they had a problem in that they needed labor and harmony among the labor force to make money. They came up with a business model. And the business model was slavery."

Mason went on to describe the thinking around how slavery and justice could coexist. "Thomas Jefferson, talking about slavery said, 'We have a wolf by the ear; we cannot hold on to him but we cannot safely turn him loose.' On the one scale we have justice, and on the other we have self-preservation."

Self-preservation, Mason said, was almost built into the system. "Slavery did two things. It dehumanized black people, and it drove a wedge between poor white people and poor black people." As Mason saw it, the establishment secured a status quo by convincing poor whites that they had more in common with rich whites than slaves.

Even after emancipation, the legacy of slavery was preserved through more sophisticated means. "Slavery morphs into Jim Crow, which was specifically designed to put black men in jail, which it did. So they could rent them out to businesses that used to use slaves. It was slavery by another name. Then, Jim Crow morphed into the war on drugs. It's all the same business model is the point."

Whether it's unemployment, incarceration, deaths from violent crime, or high infant mortality rates in the black community, by Mason's analysis, "it's all a consequence of this business model." It's also archaic with devastating consequences for all. "It's expensive, destroys neighborhoods, and puts crime on everybody's doorstep. We're kind of stuck in this business model."

The Five-Fifths Agenda, he said, offers an antidote for this vicious cycle. "We find these hidden stars, these young black men who graduate from high school but are not really predicted to finish college. We have a process to identify these hidden stars, meaning they have the grit that it takes to succeed. We put them in this rigorous program and in five years we turn them into teachers, and put them back into the schools they came from to begin that process all over again so that more and more hidden stars become less and less hidden over time."

Mason concedes that cities and school systems have seen many a well-meaning leader launch many a well-intentioned program to help black men live more productive lives—most with unremarkable results. What those programs lacked is what gives Five-Fifths its power: "The key is to do it at HBCUs," Mason said. "Because HBCUs are the only institutions that are mission driven to take on the wolf," or developing young blacks rather than socially and economically marginalizing them.

Mason put it another way: "We help them understand the wolf, help them survive and succeed in spite of the wolf, and enable them to go back into these schools where the wolf is doing the most damage and enable young people in these schools to deal better with the wolf."

The timing for Mason's idea, it seemed, was fortuitous. As the metrics for the Five-Fifths Agenda tracked with university expectations, the Obama administration launched My Brother's Keeper, an initiative aimed at reversing negative social trends for young men of color. But as Mason said, "We've had as many challenges with this administration in terms of the future of HBCUs as past administrations, even though he's a black president. Part of the challenge is that people are saying you've got a black president so you don't need black schools anymore. And the other problem is that I'm not sure he really understands that America is not postracial yet."

Mason offered an example. "Obama's pushing community colleges, and in Louisiana they are pushing community colleges. For them it's all about developing a workforce, and it also gives students some kind of degree. The problem is that in Louisiana, for instance, by raising the admission standards and cutting the need-based aid and so forth, they are in fact pushing more kids into community college. People assume that you go on to a four-year degree from a community college, but what they are not telling you is that if you start at a community college and not a four-year campus, then your chances of getting a four-year degree go down dramatically. In Louisiana, the community college graduation rate is like two or three or four percent. So you're putting these black kids into community colleges and not letting four-year schools who know how to handle them work with them."

Among HBCUs, Southern University was an anomaly: while other universities were individual entities, Southern had a community college and two four-year schools, as well as a law school and an agricultural center. Its classification as a system kept it afloat when the state legislature raised admission standards in 2011. Many assumed the changes would mean a death knell for a school like Southern without rigorous admissions standards. But Mason said the university's multitiered structure worked to its advantage. "If a student is not eligible for Southern University, we don't reject them," he said. "We just admit them into the community college and they take their classes and live on the four-year campus. When they earn eighteen credit hours and take care of all their developmental work, they automatically go into the four-year degree. That saved us really. We pulled in six hundred-plus kids this year that we probably would have lost."

But Mason was hardly immune to the politics swirling around higher education. Prior to joining Southern in 2010, he spent a decade as president of Jackson State University. In Mississippi, Mason clashed bitterly with the state's black legislators when he proposed merging Alcorn State University, Mississippi Valley State University, and Jackson State University into a single institution called Jacobs State University. His rationale was that steep cuts in state funding would disproportionately hurt the state's already financially fragile HBCUs. Mason's proposal called for revamping Jackson State University to specialize in liberal arts and postbachelor science studies, while Mississippi Valley State and Alcorn State would focus on service learning and traditional degrees, respectively. The plan, estimated to slash some $35 million from the state budget, cast Mason as an ally of the state's Republican governor, Haley Barbour, an ardent champion of merging Mississippi's HBCUs. "One strong HBCU is better than three weak ones," Mason liked to say, while the state's Black Caucus labeled him a traitor. All of this despite the fact that the state's HBCUs would be awarded half a billion dollars during seventeen consecutive years as part of the so-called Ayers settlement of a long-running lawsuit that found that the state had discriminated against these institutions in its funding.

"The HBCU president has the toughest job in higher ed," Mason said. "We've got the same expectations, but not even near the resources of the people you're competing with. Remember, HBCUs are just institutional reflections of the people they were built to serve. So you're looking at the cumulative effect of the lack of wealth and inability to generate wealth over time. You're looking at the inability to tap into alum wealth because, relatively speaking, there is no alum wealth. LSU can screw up five or six times and survive it because its sports foundation gives them millions per year to get through the hard times."

Mason was counting on the Five-Fifths Agenda to put some wind at his back. But admittedly, he was having a tough time being heard in Washington. In 2010, he served on an advisory board under Dr. John Wilson, director of the White House Initiative on Black Colleges, tasked with increasing black male bachelor's graduates. He was able to leverage those board contacts to pitch his idea inside the Beltway, and eventually the White House showed interest. But all that's dissipated now, he said, as the field has become crowded with nonprofits with a black male focus. "Everybody is trying to get in the black male space now because it's in vogue," he said. "But you have to understand it's going to take a generation. Which is why you need an institutional base—you need institutions that will outlive people to pick up the work and keep doing it over time."

At a recent meeting of black college administrators in Washington, D.C., Mason was asked by Dr. William Harvey, president of Hampton University, to present his Five-Fifths Agenda for America program to Arne Duncan, the U.S. secretary of education.

"Ron is here to talk about the four-fifths," Harvey introduced.

The perceived slight was embarrassing, but Mason kept his cool. "Hey, man," he deadpanned. "You forgot a fifth."

A Morehouse University dancer at halftime during the
Battle of the Bands at the annual AT&T Nation's
Football Classic game, in which Howard University
competes against Morehouse University at RFK Stadium
in Washington, D.C.

(*Phillip Peters/NewSport/Corbis*)

CHAPTER 15

A ROGUE REVISITED

YVETTE JOHNSON, NOW A MIDDLE-AGED PRO-fessional living in a major city, recalled the moment like it was yesterday: sitting in the backseat of her father's car as they drove along a country road near Jacksonville, Florida. Cruising along in the warm afternoon air, Yvette decided to seize the peaceful father-daughter moment and revisit a touchy household topic: establishing her own economic independence. Yvette was only ten years old, but she wanted a job badly. As she pressed her case, she realized the car had slowed down, until finally, it came to a complete stop. Yvette paused midsentence and noticed her father pointing outside, and her eyes followed his finger to a cotton field stretching out infinitely into the horizon. "You wanna work?" her father said, clearly exasperated. "Go on out there and pick some cotton."

Throughout her young life, Yvette had heard the horrific stories of slaves and their children who labored from sunup till nightfall doing the backbreaking work of picking cotton. She had heard about the sore and often bloody fingertips caused by prickly cotton bolls, how nasty green worms feeding on the cotton leaves could on contact blister your whole body, and about the poisonous snakes that lurked invisibly in the high, dense fields. The thought of such hazards was enough to silence Yvette. "Your ancestors had to do that kind of hard work," she heard her father say. "I don't want you working yet because that's my responsibility. Your only job is to go to school and get an education."

Yvette hailed from a proud lineage of formally educated Floridians, with strong roots to historically black colleges. Her mother graduated from Florida A&M University, while her father was an alumnus of Tuskegee University. Her paternal grandparents had met in the 1940s while students at Edward Waters College, a private liberal arts school in Jacksonville. Edward Waters, Florida's oldest private institution of higher education, was founded by the African Episcopal Church in 1866 to educate freed slaves and stood as the symbol of black hope and ambition in Yvette's hometown of Jacksonville, thanks partly to the late black millionaire entrepreneur and philanthropist Abraham Lincoln Lewis. A major benefactor of Edward Waters, Lewis was the great-grandfather of Johnnetta B. Cole, Spelman College's first African American president, and president of Bennett College.

Yvette's family boasted a slew of other college-educated aunts and uncles who had successful careers in various professions. Her aunt was the first African American elected to Jacksonville's city council, and her grandfather was a district judge (extremely fair-skinned, he had secured his career passing as a white man). "Education was always seen as a tool to propel you into whatever you wanted to do," said Yvette, who traveled in Europe extensively during high school. "It was not the only thing you used, but definitely part of the arsenal. It was never a question for me *whether* I was going to college. It was *where* I was going to college. Not going was not an option."

After graduating high school in 1982, Yvette went off to Dillard University. A few years prior, Yvette's older brother had gone to predominantly white University of Florida, but its sprawling size overwhelmed her, and even he conceded that he mostly "felt like a number" at the school. Her first choice was Howard University, in Washington, D.C., because of its prestigious reputation and location further north in the nation's capital. But her mother shot down that idea. Yvette's dad had recently passed away, and her mother felt more comfortable with Yvette attending a smaller, structured, tight-knit environment in the South, where there were already some family ties. Yvette laughed at the memory: "My mother figured I'd have less ability to wander around and get into trouble. But she sent me to school in New Orleans! C'mon!"

At Dillard, Yvette stepped onto a campus—aesthetically reminiscent of a Southern plantation, with Romanesque columns and neoclassical buildings—populated by bright students from middle-class and affluent families with a similar social pedigree. There were third- and fourth-generation college students who hailed from Jack and Jill, or whose parents belonged to secretive societies such as the Masons or Eastern Star. Yvette, a Delta Teen in high school, went on to pledge the sorority as a sophomore at Dillard. They all greeted her warmly. But unlike many of her classmates who seemed to tout their status as the next wave of the black social elite, Yvette viewed her privileged upbringing as a weighty obligation toward black advancement and public service.

"My mom and dad made it clear that we were not wealthy, and they'd worked hard for everything we had," she said, a biology major at Dillard. "But there were a bunch of little bratty kids there [at Dillard] and some seemed there to be babysat rather than educated." To Yvette, the standard-bearers for an elite African American family were the Coles, owners of Jacksonville's Afro-American Life Insurance Company. Yvette's mother worked for years at Afro-American as an assistant to Johnnetta B. Cole's mother, the company's vice president; to blacks in Jacksonville, and in Florida generally, the Cole family's wealth, connections, and professional achievement were the stuff of legend. For example, it was Johnnetta's oldest sister, MaVynee Betsch, an opera singer who lived in Europe, who had sparked Yvette's interest in traveling abroad during high school.

These days, Yvette, a sales manager for a nutritional medical company, cherishes her years at Dillard; learning with some of the nation's brightest black students under the tutelage of generally en-gaged professors with high expectations; the camaraderie forged in classrooms, athletic games, and Greek life that has remained strong some three decades later. "There is a perception that black schools don't bring value, and that's tragic," she said. "We are chipping away at a great source of wealth in our community; support systems that can carry and nurture us for the rest of our lives are being under-mined. We so want to forget the past that we are losing our founda-tion. We're so hell bent on assimilating into the white world that we have forgotten what made us who we are."

Much of who we are today was forged on black college campuses, where student activists organized and fought battles connected to the well-being of the race. In the 1960s, these fights put academic pursuits at risk, as students demonstrated in marches, sit-ins, and rallies that often landed participants in jail. The result is that many successful blacks who attended college during the civil rights move-ment, yet somehow escaped being on its front lines, still carry a sense of shame and regret.

"Senate Confirms Mel Watt as Fannie Mae, Freddie Mac Reg-ulator." It had taken the sixty-eight-year-old Watt, a veteran black

U.S. congressman from North Carolina, woefully long to be confirmed into that role. At least a year had passed since Watt's hearings had begun, during which he had time to reflect on his life's achievements and losses, including a decision made nearly half a century ago that continued to haunt him.

"I had scholarships to Talladega and Tuskegee, but the last place in the world I wanted to go was Alabama," Watt said. "So when I finished high school in 1963, I went to the University of North Carolina-Chapel Hill. On the first day of school I had three white roommates and by the end of the day, all of them were gone. I was one of thirteen black students accepted to Chapel Hill in a class of about two thousand, and at the time, there were lots of street demonstrations and sit-ins. I was a product of that era, and along with it came tough choices."

Watt paused. "As a student, it was very difficult because the decisions you made came with great consequences if you got involved in demonstrating. For instance, if you missed three classes, it was an automatic failure. So it had substantial impact on all of us, in many ways. One of my friends was one of the brightest in our class, and he got involved in the movement, missed classes, and took an exam and scored a ninety-seven, and they still failed him. That was the rule at the time. You were expected to be in class. It left many of us torn. It may be one of the untold stories of the civil rights movement."

He continued. "I still carry a lot of guilt about not being involved in the movement. It was a beautiful thing to observe. A lot of my friends went to jail. We were so poor, I had to go to school. I couldn't flunk out. I remember—this must have been in the late fifties—my mother telling my brother, don't you get involved in these things. Then she'd put on the TV later that night, and there'd he be on the screen. I think it colored my attitude about getting involved. I thought there was a role that everybody was playing; you could either be thoroughly immersed in the movement or thoroughly immersed in education. The choice created a great ambivalence among everybody.

"It was the toughest decision I had to make in my life. And then years later, I end up in Congress with John Lewis. Every year John takes a group of folk to the Edmund Pettus Bridge for the Civil Rights Pilgrimage. The first time I went was in 1995. I broke down and cried on that bridge. I had all these remembrances.

"It was the first time I ever realized that I carried a degree of guilt over my decision. That's why I love John Lewis. To me, not being involved in the movement had always registered as a selfish decision. I was still doing a lot of second-guessing. Like I said, the last place I wanted to go in 1963 was Alabama. Now, here I am the beneficiary of those who did it. Sometimes I feel like I am now required to produce the dividends of the decisions I made. To pay penance, so to speak, for those decisions. John Lewis got his head beat in, and was arrested several times. He's a hero and I'm a beneficiary of his commitment to the struggle."

We are all, on some level, beneficiaries. But we have also been decidedly acquiescent during this less violent but similarly crucial hour—a time when the pillars of black economic and social advancement are crumbling. Where, now, is that old sense of urgency to crusade for our children and their future? Even during our most oppressive years of slavery, we understood that our only real passport to freedom was a solid education—that the study of the sciences and humanities was an essential currency for building strong families and communities in a nation rigged against our well-being.

What happened? Now, in this über Information Age, governed by software designers and engineers and mathematicians, our freedoms have become even more intricately linked to a high-quality education. But instead of alarms, we hear nary a sound from the black community about the cyclical crises that threaten our next generation from competing in a new world order. There is no discernible outrage over the fact that, according to the U.S. Census Bureau, the average black college graduate earns $18,000 more per year than those who don't have college degrees. During the '50s and '60s, the John Lewises of this nation were relentless in their courage, going toe-to-toe with police nightsticks, water hoses, and attack dogs. Their selflessness was heroic.

Ronald Carter, the president of Johnson C. Smith University, talked about the need to galvanize black educators and protest policies in Washington, D.C. He was particularly concerned that JCSU's retention rate dropped from 72 to 54 percent after some 130 students were denied Direct PLUS loans due to changes in credit standards; that in those private universities supported by the United Negro College Fund, the changes resulted in a $50 million decline in revenue. As Carter put it in an opinion piece published in the higher ed newsmagazine *Diverse: Issues in Higher Education*: " . . . armed with the facts, we should take our message to the White House and demonstrate, through what I have called an 'Intellectual March on Washington,' how current policies have failed. As leaders of higher education institutions, it's critical that we look at the logic model coming out of Washington and summon the collective courage to push back against wrong-headed policies, based on statistical evidence. And, at the grassroots level, we must mobilize our constituencies, inform our political candidates and vote intelligently."

Julianne Malveaux, the celebrated African American economist, had spoken candidly, too, about the grave challenges facing HBCU leaders. After retiring as president of Bennett College, Malveaux spoke frequently about the various plagues suffered by HBCUs; from paltry endowments, to draconian cuts in federal aid, to the tangle of bureaucratic red tape from higher ed accrediting bodies. But in her poignant 2013 essay, "Is There a War on HBCUs?" published in *Essence*, Malveaux also conceded that some HBCU leaders are afraid to speak truth to power for fear of retribution. "During my tenure I felt as if I had a muzzle on my mouth when I wanted to respond to some fiscal policy changes and some did not agree."

If HBCUs are at war, as Malveaux's essay so adroitly posed as a scenario, I believe the war is also against ourselves. It is a war over how HBCU leaders can reclaim their high sense of mission and values and "yes" courage that once guided these institutions; how they might detour off a dead-end street of vendor contracts to family and friends, personal valets and travel junkets, of disengaged adjunct faculty and low student expectations; of trying to reel in rich white donors while letting black alum off the hook. It is a war over whether to embrace new innovative practices or stumble along in anachronistic business models that virtually ensured extinction; to have the guts, as Spelman's Beverly Daniel Tatum proved, to jettison organized sports when the tab becomes too high.

We know what the alternative looks like. For example, competitive pressures, along with desegregation court orders, have already forced HBCUs to broaden their student base beyond black students. Several HBCUs, such as Jackson State in Mississippi and Lincoln University in Missouri, are already enrolling record numbers of white students. Over the past three decades, the number of white students at HBCUs has skyrocketed 67 percent, from 21,000 to nearly 35,000. If you visit the campus of Bluefield State College in West Virginia, for example, an HBCU once known as Bluefield Colored Institute, you'll find a campus that's nearly 90 percent white.

There was a rich—if not long forgotten—tradition of HBCUs fighting at moments like this. In the 1920s, there were uprisings at Hampton University when students protested against Ku Klux Klan members working as faculty, and at Lincoln University where the state's governor had ousted a popular black president for raising the university's academic standards. There was the time, too, back when students at Florida A&M learned that the university's president, W. H. A. Howard, lacked a college degree and staged a boycott by withdrawing from classes until the board installed a new president.

Among the more dramatic protests was in 1924, when Fayette McKenzie, the white president of Fisk University, found his oppressive policies toward students challenged by students and faculty alike. In *I'll Find a Way or Make One*, journalist Juan Williams and Dwayne Ashley, then president of the Thurgood Marshall College Fund, detail McKenzie's control tactics, from banning the student government association, to shutting down the student newspaper, to prohibiting interaction between the sexes by not permitting fraternities and sororities on campus. As the authors state, "McKenzie also instituted a tyrannical student code of conduct: and while the rules partially addressed the belief held by many whites that blacks were not able to control their sexual urges or behavior, they also satisfied McKenzie's own puritanical sense of propriety." Among those outraged by McKenzie's actions was none other than Fisk alum W. E. B. Du Bois, who upon hearing reports, joined students in pushing for his resignation. After months of fiery student demonstrations, which included student protesters being arrested, McKenzie grudgingly resigned in 1925.

One might argue that, almost a century later, Renee Higginbotham-Brooks's actions at Howard University did not quite measure up to this storied history. After all, Higginbotham-Brooks's indictment of the university's leadership was never intended for public consumption but rather for trustees' eyes only. Even more, Higginbotham-Brooks was a decidedly solo act; if there were others supporting her, the public never heard from them.

What was less arguable, though, is that when Renee Higginbotham-Brooks wrote her infamous letter to the board of trustees, Howard University desperately needed an agitator, someone willing to step up and call bullshit on the powers that be. Howard had become through the years an ailing giant, lumbering along on its laurels as a black intellectual powerhouse. But it had become harder to proclaim such glory: its finances were buckling under bloated expenses; its dormitories, classrooms, and administration buildings had fallen into serious disrepair; its business office was disorganized and inefficient. Even worse, the university's governing body seemed paralyzed as it watched one of the world's great institutions fall from grace.

Indeed, the depth of Howard's woes caught boosters flat-footed. "In Surprise Move, President of Howard University Resigns as Budget Troubles Loom," the headline ran in the *New York Times*. It was October 2, 2013, and the crises at Howard had gained new momentum as it splashed deeper into public view. As the *Chronicle of Higher Education* reported: "Mr. Ribeau's retirement comes on the heels of a troubled year for Howard, in which deans and trustees publicly blasted leaders of the historically black university for mismanagement, falling enrollment, and a hospital in financial straits." The *Washington Post*, in a lengthy feature on the departure, wrote: " . . . the announcement of Ribeau's exit came nearly four months after a rupture between the board's two top leaders emerged, sending shock waves through the university community." The *Post* also noted that Ribeau's contract had been extended through June 2015, and that the announcement followed a "tense" meeting of the board. As *Inside Higher Ed* put it: "Amid the various controversies, there has been no indication that a change was imminent at Howard."

Colby King, a *Washington Post* editor, Howard alum, and close friend of board member Frank Savage, used an invitation to speak at a board meeting to rally greater engagement and accountability. "You should not even be on this board if you are not about the three Gs," he said. "Give money, get money, or get the hell off the board."

Howard's board of trustees has boasted a pantheon of great leaders through the years, black and white alike. Most of them, notably, have been men—Colin Powell, Vernon Jordan, Ken Lewis, Douglas Wilder, and Jack Kemp, to name a few. There was, within this gender gap, a noticeable irony in the fact that Howard's whistleblower was Higginbotham-Brooks, a woman. It was tempting to view this as mere coincidence, but doing so required ignoring other facts—both anecdotal and empirical—that suggest otherwise.

What was clear is that by taking on Howard's good ol' boys, Renee Higginbotham-Brooks had joined the proud legacy of Sherron Watkins, the Enron executive, who penned the infamous memo pointing out to the company's CEO Ken Lay that Enron's accounting practices were unlawful; Cynthia Cooper, the internal auditor at WorldCom, whose corporate sleuthing exposed history's largest known bookkeeping scam; Claudia Kennedy, the retired Army lieutenant general, who shed light on a culture of sexual harassment permeating the armed forces. And this list of female objectors jibed, too, with recent scientific studies that strongly suggest women to be more bound by ethics than their male colleagues in the workplace and less inclined than men to compromise their personal values—in other words, sell out—to fit in or prosper in corporate organizations.

Renee Higginbotham-Brooks certainly fits that description. But in honesty, as Christmas approached, she was not the same self-assured insider of months before. Even though she had won her battle and forced Sidney Ribeau to resign, even though Dr. Wayne A. I. Frederick, whom she really admired, had been named interim president, Higginbotham-Brooks was anything but celebratory. In fact, she seemed subdued, humbled even, by the events. While some at Howard quietly applauded her efforts, she was mostly treated as a kind of traitor, especially by the board. This stung, but she felt no regret for her actions. In the end, she was certain that her battle had been worthwhile, as Howard's board of trustees prepared to announce that Vernon Jordan was to head the university's search committee for a new president. When she showed up at board meetings, she was greeted mostly by empty stares. "I've been through a lot in my life, so trust me when I tell you: I ain't afraid of no man—or anybody else. I love Howard, and that's all that really matters."

On a late Saturday afternoon in August, Savannah Bowen, standing in the pouring rain, bid farewell to her parents, her aunt, and her two younger sisters as they drove away from Bethune Annex dormitory, her new home at Howard University. For months, Savannah had been anticipating this big moment: when she was finally free to live her life independent of her parents, when she could make some new friends, chart a fresh path on her own terms. But as the family sedan receded into traffic and disappeared from view, a feeling of loss settled darkly upon her like those thick gray clouds draping across the Washington, D.C., skies. A terrible sadness washed over her. Around her throngs of students headed festively out of the dorm into the wet streets for the annual pinning ceremony, a rite of passage for Howard freshmen. But Savannah, feeling too melancholy to participate in the event, went upstairs to her room, got in bed, and wept herself to sleep.

When she awoke, the depression had lifted, and Savannah felt certain she had made the right decision. She was at the epicenter of her family's history. She and her roommate, an introvert from a small town in North Carolina, admittedly got off to a bumpy start. The girl barely spoke a word to Savannah, preferring instead to sit in the room watching TV late into the night. Savannah tried to break through her roommate's gloomy disposition, one day even surprising her with her favorite Mr. Goodbar candy. But none of that worked—she concluded that the girl was plain homesick—and Savannah eventually stopped trying and made friends with other girls on the floor. Her favorite was a freshman named Enessa, a studious girl from East Saint Louis. They struck up a good friendship, becoming study partners and on Sundays going to church together.

Savannah, admittedly, experienced a bit of a culture shock adjusting to Howard, as she had never gone to school with mostly black kids. But she quickly grew to enjoy the feeling of being a student at

Howard. While unfamiliar to her initially, she felt a remarkable sense of peace on campus, living and learning with people who looked like her. "I really learned to love my community," she said. "I mean, it's hard to love yourself when everyone is skinny and nothing else is viewed as beautiful.

"Being at Howard, there are a lot of ways to be beautiful and to be proud. Women of all shapes and colors and sizes can be beautiful, and that was comforting to know.

"And you see black men in business suits, and dashikis and wearing hoodies, and they are beautiful, too."

Now a junior English major studying abroad in Paris, Savannah has no regrets about her decision. She has built lots of tight friendships with students from all socioeconomic backgrounds. Even more, the academics throughout have been rigorous enough to keep her challenged, and even inspired. She admits, though, that some of the courses she had taken prior to declaring her major were not quite as intellectually challenging as she was accustomed to. She mostly enjoys her English and writing professors, and has even begun considering continuing studying English in graduate school with the goal of perhaps teaching one day. What Howard University has mostly offered is something she likely would not have gotten at a predominantly white college, a more empowered and real sense of herself. "Coming here has been a step in my growth as a black person," she said. "I never had any real confidence about that; it was always someone praising because I was good, or pretending that I wasn't."

Entertainer and entrepreneur Sean "P. Diddy" Combs takes a selfie with 2014 Howard University graduates after delivering the university's commencement address. (*Jose Luis Magana/AP*)

EPILOGUE

IN THE SUMMER OF 2014, THE NEWS BROKE that Howard University had selected a new president. I got a phone call from Renee Higginbotham-Brooks. It had been several months since our last conversation, an exchange that turned tense as she recounted Howard's trustees' decision to replace her as board vice chair. Higginbotham-Brooks, who remained on the board but lacked her previous influence, tried not to sound bitter or bruised by the turn of events. "Look, this was never about me in the first place," she said. "This was about putting Howard University back on the right path. So I'm okay with whatever." But the proud talk couldn't mask her hurt feelings.

Now, though, Higginbotham-Brooks sounded decidedly cheery—and she spent the next thirty minutes or so explaining all the reasons why, mostly from voting to install forty-three-year-old Dr. Wayne Frederick as president of Howard University. The Trinidadian embodied the Howard success story: from his childhood battles with sickle cell anemia to wending his way through Howard's undergraduate and medical schools in six years with the goal of finding a cure for the illness that afflicted him. "He's the perfect choice," she said. "There's no one who better represents the future of Howard University than Dr. Frederick."

Higginbotham-Brooks said she was also elated that Addison Barry Rand, the proverbial thorn in her side, had gradually disappeared from Howard's scene. Over the past few months, since Ribeau had stepped down as Howard's president, Rand's board participation had begun to fade as the chairman's torch was passed on to Stacey J. Mobley, an attorney and former general counsel for DuPont. Rand was scaling back, too, at AARP, having recently announced his retirement.

On top of it all, she chirped, Howard's incoming class of freshmen was an impressive bunch: larger and better prepared academically than any in recent years. Some 1,600 students had enrolled at Howard, the university's largest class in fifteen years, for the 2014–2015 school year, compared to 1,596 the previous school year. Their average GPA was 3.29, and SAT scores were 1,637. "I tell you, we're back," Higginbotham-Brooks said. "Don't let anyone tell you anything different—Howard University is back!"

This was all good news for Howard, and I praised Higginbotham-Brooks for fighting for what she believed was right. Still, I couldn't help but weigh her glad tidings against other events inside the ecosystem of black higher education—events whose impact would rumble beyond Howard across the broader black college landscape. Harvard University, the standard-bearer of elite American universities, had granted admission to 170 blacks, the largest number of black students in the university's 378-year history. That number was made even more impressive by the fact that 34,295 had applied, while just over 2,000 were accepted into the 2018 class. Even more, these black students didn't hail from financially well-off families: most would receive need-based aid upwards of $40,000 to defray the university's nearly $59,000 annual cost, including tuition, room and board, and fees. For some reason, the successful luring of top black students by such elites as Harvard, Princeton, and Yale eclipsed the otherwise positive news that a handful of celebrated black scholars such as Columbia's Marc Lamont Hill, or Rutgers's Fred Bonner II, or Brown's Dr. Corey D. B. Walker were ditching those schools to join HBCUs Morehouse, Prairie View A&M, and Winston-Salem State, respectively.

In some cases, the outreach to black students was nothing less than cynical. Anyone with a social conscience, for example, had to wonder what the repercussions would be of the ultraconservative Koch brothers' foundation donating $25 million to the United Negro College Fund. Granted, HBCUs desperately needed the funding. But while Michael Lomax, president of the United Negro College Fund, vehemently defended accepting the gift ("Criticism is a small price for helping young people get the chance to realize their dream of a college education," Lomax said), his explanation failed to allay perfectly reasonable outrage from several HBCU leaders who accused the organization of selling out. As HBCU scribe Jarrett L. Carter vented in the *Huffington Post*: "So what makes us angrier? Twenty-five million dollars from conservative business owners who fix elections, suppress voters and shape policies which negatively impact millions of Black folks nationwide? Or the fact that our schools can't afford to tell the Koch brothers where to shove it?"

The aftermath of 2013 had turned the noble work of leading HBCUs into a certified blood sport—and many had begun to graciously bow out of the competition. Cheyney University's president Michelle Howard-Vital, and Beverly Daniel Tatum, president of Spelman College, had both announced plans to retire the following summer. Howard-Vital, after seven years on the job, was essentially pushed out by a board displeased by the university's declining enrollment and poor overall morale. Conversely, Tatum, fifty-nine, was leaving valiantly: she boasted a track record that included snaring nearly $160 million from Spelman alum for scholarships, faculty research, and campus infrastructure.

Xavier University's Dr. Norman Francis announced, too, that he was calling it quits after forty-six years at the helm. "I believe that the time has come to take the brightly burning torch turned over to me by the Sisters of the Blessed Sacrament and pass it on to new leadership," Francis announced. Xavier's trustees tried to give the job to New Orleans native son and former mayor Marc Morial, who was head of the National Urban League, but he wasn't interested. The university brought in Dr. C. Reynold Verret, provost and vice president of academic affairs at Savannah State University, to succeed Dr. Francis.

Tuskegee University handed its reins to Dr. Brian Johnson, an energetic forty-year-old W. E. B. Du Bois scholar. He assumed the role as the university's seventh president following Dr. Gilbert L. Rochon, who had been forced out by trustees for what was deemed poor fiscal management. Meanwhile, Southern University's president, Dr. Ronald Mason, lost the support of the board as he pushed to reorganize the university's statewide system; it voted not to extend his contract. The brightest news for Southern was that the Bayou Classic, under Dottie Belletto's leadership, was gaining momentum after a long malaise.

Several other HBCUs continued their downward slide, perhaps most notably Wilberforce University. After probing the university's operations for a year, the accrediting body, the North Central Association of Colleges and Schools, slapped Wilberforce with a "show-cause" order and gave the university until year's end to show proof that the school's academics and finances were solid enough to keep

its accreditation. For the turnaround, Wilberforce hired Dr. Algea-
nia Warren Freeman, a veteran HBCU administrator with her own
track record of controversy. While regarded as an effective, no-
nonsense administrator, Freeman also suffered a reputation among
colleagues as oftentimes divisive in her tactics to get the job done. As
the *Indianapolis Business Journal* reported about Freeman's tenure at
Martin College, where she was president before resigning in 2010:
"Her tactics drew complaints from employees who said Freeman was
overly harsh and shuffled people into jobs that made little sense.
Students protested after a popular professor was fired, and seven
members of the university's sixteen-person board of trustees resigned
in 2008, including at least two who said Freeman's methods were a
factor." Unfortunately, Wilberforce seemed to be heading the way of
Morris Brown College, which was now dragging along without accreditation, had less than fifty students, and was in the process of
selling its storied 134-year-old campus to Atlanta's economic development agency and a neighboring Baptist church to clear the way
for a new Atlanta Falcons stadium.

Indeed, the fall of HBCUs was becoming steeper and embarrassing. How to explain the foibles at Alabama State University, which
now suffered a kind of prolonged institutional paralysis? Sure, there
was the unseemly financial scandal, but the fallout seemed to grow
more bizarre each week. To succeed Joseph Silver, the university's
board tapped Gwendolyn Boyd, known for her stellar fund-raising
as president of Delta Sigma Theta sorority's national chapter. But
that relationship seemed strained almost from the start. First, there
was the odd contract clause that prohibited her from having romantic liaisons staying overnight; then came an angry letter penned by
the board chair apologizing for hiring Boyd in the first place. "While

Dr. Boyd did not create these problems, I now realize that she does not have the executive management skills to solve them," wrote Donald Watkins, a member of the university's search committee that hired Boyd. The mess at ASU had broader consequences: blaming weak governance and poor finances, Moody's Investor Services downgraded the university's credit rating.

But Renee Higginbotham-Brooks, in this moment at least, believed that Howard University had survived its darkest hour—and she sensed the clouds starting to break. She told me about how, at that last trustees' meeting, after voting to install Dr. Frederick, she shared a story with her colleagues. She told them about how she recently met former Dallas Cowboys star Michael Irvin; and how she had helped his daughter, an incoming freshman, move smoothly through the registration process, and how appreciative Irvin was for the assistance. "Whatever I can do to return the favor, just let me know," he told Higginbotham-Brooks, who, of course, was armed with a ready response. "I need you to cohost a fund-raiser with me right here in Dallas for Howard's new president, Dr. Wayne Frederick," she shot back. When she told the fellow trustees at a board meeting that Irvin had agreed to cohost a fund-raiser that fall, there was none of the hoopla that typically occurs with such announcements. That didn't surprise Higginbotham-Brooks one bit. The wounds between Higginbotham-Brooks and fellow trustees were simply too deep, and were unlikely to ever heal.

Several months later, Higginbotham-Brooks sat for breakfast at the Fairmont Hotel in Washington, D.C., the place where she overheard the infamous conversation between Rand and Ribeau—and which set in motion her campaign to save Howard. Dressed conservatively in a lavender dress and pearl necklace, she had an early trustees' meeting and then, later that morning, was scheduled to take the stage at Howard for the official convocation of Dr. Frederick.

Over eggs, toast, and coffee, Higginbotham-Brooks could feel the clock ticking, that her days on the board were numbered. She had already been pushed out of her most important roles; she was no longer vice chair, nor chair of the development committee. And her term was set to expire in July. "I'm not going to quit," she said, "but I figure they'll ask me to leave. They'll have to push me off."

Later that morning, onstage at Cramton Auditorium, Higginbotham-Brooks donned a royal-blue cap and gown amid the pomp and pageantry of Dr. Frederick's convocation. In this moment, none of these board disputes seemed to matter. Renee Higginbotham-Brooks looked regal and triumphant, flanked by her fellow trustees as they held crossed hands, singing the old Howard University fight song:

> *Reared against the eastern sky*
> *Proudly there on hilltop high*
> *Far above the lake so blue*
> *Stands old Howard firm and true*

ACKNOWLEDGMENTS

This book was born from the generosity of more people than I could ever thank in this space. I am blessed with numerous friends and colleagues who were always patient and willing to talk through this work with me, whose ideas, insight, and encouragement spirited the book to completion. To each I owe a debt of gratitude. I especially thank my brilliant editor, Tracy Sherrod, whose blend of intellect, passion, and grace helped bring form to a complex, often unwieldy topic. Along with the thrill of a work completed is also the bittersweetness of fewer chats with a supremely gifted book editor.

I am also grateful to Tracy's lieutenant, assistant editor Laura Brown, for working to ensure seamless movement of copy and communiqués; and general counsel Victor Hendrickson for his exacting eye and collegial spirit. Many thanks, too, to relentless photo researcher Kathy Moore, and fact-checker Angela Vogel Daley.

From inception, this author also benefited from the sage guidance and representation of literary agent Leah Nathans Spiro, whose commitment to this book—and my work overall—is often humbling. Thank you, Leah, for so generously sharing your expertise, camaraderie, and friendship.

Also invaluable to this project were the administrators, faculty, students, and alumni at dozens of historically black colleges and universities, including Cleve Edwards, Natalie Moore, and Jonathan Webb. Much appreciation, too, to my home campus of Johnson C. Smith University in Charlotte, N.C., whose transformative vision inspired and informed this work; thank you to JCSU president Dr. Ronald L. Carter for trusting me with a front row seat at one of the nation's most innovative HBCUs; Dr. Elfred Anthony Pinkard, chief operating officer, for helping to shape my understanding and appreciation for the important mission of HBCUs; and colleague and friend Keisha Talbot Johnson for reading and critiquing my early drafts. There were many JCSU students, too, whose opinions and experiences, while not cited directly, nonetheless infuse these pages, most notably Austin Jacque, Akira Carr, Andronica Klaas, Dana Harris, Daniel Rocha Herrera, Dineo Seakamela, DeShauna Selby, Janelle S. Martin, and Jeremiah Chapman.

Thank you to my family, Kimberly Minter Walker, Robert Pryor, Louise Springer, and Shawn Springer. I am deeply appreciative always of my loving wife Robyn Springer, whose support and encouragement help make such work possible, and to my sons Ronald, Robert, and Randall, whose dreams and future give purpose to my work and life.

And thank you foremost to God, from whom all blessings flow.

ABOUT THE AUTHOR

AWARD-WINNING JOURNALIST RON STODGHILL has worked for the *New York Times, Time, Business Week,* and *Savoy,* for which he was editor in chief. He was a Nieman Fellow at Harvard University. Stodghill is the author of *Redbone* and his work has been anthologized in *Brotherman,* and has appeared in *Slate, Essence, Black Enterprise,* and *Ebony.* He is also a professor at Johnson C. Smith University, an HBCU in Charlotte, North Carolina, where he lives with his wife and three sons.